DAWN OF LABOR

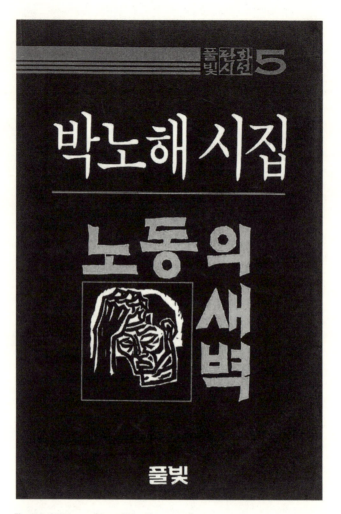

The original 1984 cover of *Dawn of Labor*. The poetry collection, written by a twenty-seven-year-old factory worker, pierced the heart of an era. Despite a ban by the authoritarian government, the collection sold a million copies and left an indelible mark on Korea's literary history. Park Nohae wrote the manuscript with pencil on tissue paper, and a critic published it without revealing the identity of the author. The literary world was instantly ignited by the book's vivid portrayal of the suffering of ten million workers, a group all but forgotten by the Korean society at large. Park Nohae, who became known as "the faceless poet," was soon wanted by the police. Many college students read his poems and gave up their privileges, entering the factories as workers themselves and building a workers' liberation movement from within. The poems from *Dawn of Labor* became widely known as songs and plays as well, and it remains the poetry collection with the most number of poems made into songs. On the twentieth anniversary of its publication, in 2004, an album of *Dawn of Labor* songs was released and a concert was held. In the 1990s, some of the poems were translated in the United States, Japan, and Europe, and these translated poems served as texts to understand the Korean society. Four decades after its first publication, *Dawn of Labor* is still showing us the power of poetry.

HAWAI'I STUDIES ON KOREA

DAWN OF LABOR

Park Nohae

*Translated by Brother Anthony of Taizé and
Cheehyung Harrison Kim*

With essays by Janet Poole and Brother Anthony

University of Hawai'i Press, Honolulu
and
Center for Korean Studies, University of Hawai'i

This book is published with the support of the Literature Translation Institute of Korea (LTI Korea)

© 2024 University of Hawaiʻi Press

All rights reserved

Printed in the United States of America

First printed, 2024

Published by arrangement with Slow Walking Press. Originally published in Korea by Pulbitbooks.

Library of Congress Cataloging-in-Publication Data
Names: Pak, No-hae, author. | Kim, Cheehyung Harrison, translator. | Anthony, of Taizé, Brother, translator, writer of added commentary. | Poole, Janet, writer of added commentary.
Title: Dawn of labor / Park Nohae ; translated by Brother Anthony of Taizé and Cheehyung Harrison Kim ; with essays by Janet Poole and Brother Anthony.
Other titles: Nodong ŭi saebyŏk. English
Description: Honolulu : University of Hawaiʻi Press, 2024. | Series: Hawaiʻi studies on Korea
Identifiers: LCCN 2023029862 (print) | LCCN 2023029863 (ebook) | ISBN 9780824894047 (hardback ; acid-free paper) | ISBN 9780824895648 (trade paperback ; acid-free paper) | ISBN 9780824896447 (epub) | ISBN 9780824896454 (kindle edition) | ISBN 9780824896430 (pdf)
Subjects: LCSH: Pak, No-hae—Criticism and interpretation. | LCGFT: Poetry. | Literary criticism. | Essays.
Classification: LCC PL992.62.N64 N613 2024 (print) | LCC PL992.62.N64 (ebook) | DDC 895.71/4—dc23/eng/20230731
LC record available at https://lccn.loc.gov/2023029862
LC ebook record available at https://lccn.loc.gov/2023029863

The Center for Korean Studies, established in 1972, coordinates and develops resources for the study of Korea at the University of Hawaiʻi. The series Hawaiʻi Studies on Korea, published jointly by the Center for Korean Studies and the University of Hawaiʻi Press, aims to advance interdisciplinary engagement in social sciences, humanities, and the arts pertaining to Korea.

University of Hawaiʻi Press books are printed on acid-free paper and meet the guidelines for permanence and durability of the Council on Library Resources.

The image of the worker on the cover comes from a woodblock piece by the artist Oh Yoon.
Cover design by Hong Dongwon.

I dedicate these words,
like a round of drinks,
to my working sisters and brothers,
who, despite the bleak life of labor
with low pay and long hours,
live and act diligently
without losing hope and laughter.

Park Nohae,
in blazing May 1984

Contents

Note on Romanization, Translation, and Glossary ix

PART I   **Our Love, Our Unrelenting Life**
Heaven 3
No Way to Stop 5
A Newlywed's Diary 7
Made for Each Other 9
While I Mend the Bedding 12
How Much? 14
Where Will We Go? 16
The Han River 18
Longing 19
The Bar Wagon 20
Garibong Market 23
Calling for Fingerprints 25
English Conversation 27
Off to Rot 30
Record of My Journey with Men 33
Incomprehensible Tales 36
Becoming Wise 38

PART II   **Dawn of Labor**
Bargain Sale 43
The Dream of an Apprentice 45
Spring 47
Sleepiness 49
Working on Sunday 51
A Hand Grave 53
Maybe 56
When I Give You Up 58

vii

A Real Worker   60
For a Peaceful Evening   62
Dawn of Labor   64
No Other Way   66
Sunset   68

PART III   **For a New Land**
Love   73
The Wind to the Stones   74
Searching for Food   75
Confrontation   78
A Song about Leaving   80
Am I Drifting?   82
Samcheong Reeducation Camp I   84
Mother   89
A Beautiful Confession   92
I Am Nothing Special   95
Walls   97
Illusions   99

Dawn of Labor **in Korean**   101

Glossary   231

The Worker-Poet in Mass Culture
Janet Poole   241

Poet Militant, Poet Inspirational
Brother Anthony of Taizé   249

About Park Nohae   261

About the Translators and Contributor   267

Note on Romanization, Translation, and Glossary

The Revised Romanization system is used in this book. Various Korean words are romanized but untranslated, to preserve their significance. These words, along with culturally important terms, are italicized in the poems and explained in the glossary. The original Korean-language poems are also presented, following the English translations, so that those who read Korean can appreciate the author's mastery of language.

PART I

Our Love, Our Unrelenting Life

Heaven

The rope of survival for my family of three is held by
    my boss,
so he's my heaven.

When I am at the hospital cradling a hand crushed in
    the *press,*
the doctor can patch me up or leave me crippled,
so he's my heaven.

When we are dragged to the police for organizing a union
after two months without pay,
the officer who threatens to lock us up,
though we've committed no crime,
is always a frightening heaven.

The judges and lawyers,
who can turn us into criminals or set us free,
are a dreadful heaven.

The bureaucrats, sitting in government offices,
who can make us or break us,
are a fearsome heaven.

People high up, people with power, people with money
all appear to be heaven.

No, they are indeed heaven,
the heaven of darkness controlling our lives.

Will I ever be heaven
for someone somewhere?
I have lived only at the bottom, powerless.
But for one person,
our insanely beautiful baby,
who now begins to walk,
I may be a small, unsteady heaven.

We, too, want to become heaven.
Not a dark clouded heaven
that presses down,
but a clear blue heaven
over a world where we lift one another.

No Way to Stop

Quickly, quickly . . .
Eating my breakfast quickly,
chasing a packed bus,
walking in a hurry,
changing into work clothes in a flash,
zoom, zing,
feverishly I spin all day.

A long line for a meal.
Holding the tray up to my mouth,
gulping down the rice mixed in soup.
In the restroom to piss but no time for more.
A fast burn of the cigarette,
then returning for an extended shift.
Frenzy like a battlefield,
the machines turn and roar.
I am too spent to keep up
with the disco beats
blasting from the speakers.

Rushing out the factory gates,
faces listless and steeped in sweat.
Scattering into darkness
without goodbyes.
I walk up a hillside, panting.

I am a spinning top that spins when whipped,
a load of laundry in a washing machine,
wrung ever drier as the machine turns faster.
Each day, each year, until death,
spinning mindlessly,
in a mindlessly changing world.
Gone are my eyes' shine, my smile, and my thoughts,
all lost in the midst of speed.

I run with all my strength,
but the farther I go, the more distant I am,
like a parrotbill following a stork,
like a rooster following a peacock,
like running after a car barefoot.
Hands and feet can't stop until death.
I want to walk, I want to sit,
but more frightening than any whip
is the fact that I must live.
A worker's fate
knows no stopping unless it meets death.

Today and tomorrow,
the farther we go, the faster we run,
the less we own and the tighter our belts become.
In our welfare country of the Republic of Korea,
prospering higher,
developing faster,
we are the workers
spinning in the same spot.

A Newlywed's Diary

At the end of a long week of work,
trudging through the coldness of dawn,
I come home,
holding my frosty heart.
My wife is not here.
She has already left for the factory.

I sigh over our long separation
during the week's labor
and release the bitter smoke of a cigarette.
I pick up her nightdress, hurriedly thrown aside,
and my eyes begin to tear from the scent of her body,
which has spent these nights alone.

I open my eyes in pain,
awaking from deep sleep, still uncontrollably tired.
Returning from night work, her body cold,
she lies on me and strokes my chest.
With her loving kiss,
my body comes back to life.

Filled with sweet words and sweet touches,
our one night is too short
for sharing a meal
and talking about the week.

The day breaks, and we part again.
We dread the morning,
when we become machines and return into labor.

Turning around with hope, full of each other's love,
looking ahead in unity,
our penurious love, our newlywed's song.

Made for Each Other

Why I love you, my dear,
is not because you're pretty,
not because I feel sorry about your hardened hands.
As for looking good, nobody compares to a TV star.
As for glamour, nobody rivals the women of *Jongno*.
As for sophistication, exuding elegance and charm,
nobody comes close to college girls.
As for amazement in bed,
nobody matches the women of the *Five-Eight-Eight District*.
As for service, nobody is better than a maid.
As for cooking or arranging flowers,
nobody competes with the experts.
Yet I really adore you.
The longer I live,
the more I know that you are the best in the world.
I adore you so so much.

I come home drunk with friends.
For days, I roam from house to house, past midnight.
But your concern for my health revives my spirit.
Three years into our marriage, I haven't bought you a dress.
We haven't yet gone out for *jjajangmyeon,*
and you've used the same bottle of lotion for more than
    a year.
But I'm fond of you because you smile like a spring flower.

When Saturday comes, you bring home a drove of friends,
turning me into a cook, though I'm weak and tired.
Nowadays, washing clothes, changing the briquette fire, and
    making kimchi
have become my lot,
but as long as you're with me, I'm ripping happy.

When I'm indolent or insincere,
your merciless criticism is frightening.
When I'm despondent and weary,
you restore my life with embrace.
I wonder what part of your small body
releases all that love and strength.
As you sleep, I open your blouse, stare at your breasts, and
    laugh like a fool.

We met as *factory girl* and *factory boy*,
unschooled and bruised,
standing up from the depth of sorrow and despair.
You and I are made for each other.
We shall smash, with our love,
the dark fate of workers in the bright Republic of Korea,
who wither away from low wages, long hours, and
    oppression.
Like the stars at night,
like a flowing stream,
like wildflowers,
we dream of living peacefully together.
Although we may not live to see the end,
beneath the savage hooves,
and although we might be swept away,
without letting out a scream,
by the terrifying and swirling turbid river,
we still travel this road with joy.
How I adore you, my dear, with all my tears.

If you and I shatter on the way,
we shall live on within the multitude,
beyond the history of death.
Each spring, we'll bloom throughout the land,
you as forsythia, I as azalea,
kissing in the spring breeze, talking about the old days,
watching the young workers,
who come to the mountain after their shift, in pairs,
who laugh loudly with azaleas and forsythias in their
 mouths,
and we will fade away as teardrops, my dear.
How I adore you.
My comrade, my partner,
I love you more than anything.
I adore you madly.

While I Mend the Bedding

While I mend the layers of the bedding,
while I wash my underclothes,
I beat my chest out of shame.

Although she comes home after work from the factory just
    like me,
I used to make my wife bring me food, water, and clothes,
even as she, until past midnight, washed the dishes, cleaned
    the room, and
fixed the lid of the pepper paste jar.

Since I began unionizing with fellow workers,
the arrogant and tyrannical acts of the factory owner
have been committed by me on my wife, in the name of
    the husband.
I recognize this with sorrow.

Society has taught me that
men give orders and women obey.
As I gnawed on my wife, bit by bit,
I was an earnest model worker.

While forming a labor union,
I saw clearly that their praises and awards
were the sound of a bell tied to a cat's tail,

that their care and love for the workers
were empty as cotton candy.

Like the appalling pursuit of profit,
packaged as handy theory, absolute authority, and common
    sense,
I, too, had become a dictator,
exploiting my wife at home.

In practice, as the struggle grows,
I begin to excrete the residue.
A worker is not a profit-making machine,
and my wife is not my servant.
She is a friend and a partner to be loved equally,
our relationship based on
trust, respect, and democracy.
I wait for my wife to come home after extra work.
Mending the layers of the bedding,
I push the needle of painful awakening.

How Much?

My stuttering cousin, the dyer,
lost ten years of severance pay to a swindler
promising a job in the Middle East,
so he killed himself.
One million *won* is
the cost of my sick mother's visit to the hospital,
the cost of a wedding for my twenty-nine-year-old
    spinsterish sister.
Ten million won is
how much I would make in ten years.
A hundred million won is
a distant rainbow, many rivers and hills away,
something I can't imagine if I worked two lifetimes.
My life is worth four thousand won a day.
How much are you worth?
They say my boss spends a million won on an evening's
    drinks.
They say his dog food costs five thousand won a day.
They say there is a woman who reigns over three hundred
    billion won.
My cousin the dyer kills himself over one million, two
    hundred thousand won.
My little brother goes to the factory at the age of
    sixteen.

My, oh my . . .
Our life, our love, our existence . . .
How much are we worth? How much?

Where Will We Go?

Where will we go
on this dazzling azure day in May?
Can't remember the last time I had a day off.
My girl, Jeongsun, has an extra shift today, again.
Where will I go?
The pro baseball broadcast has ended,
so watching TV is boring.
Spent a few coins at the arcade . . .
I feel tired to even wander these streets.
I want to drink a cold draft beer,
see a movie at the theater,
and go to a disco club,
but I've already withdrawn fifty thousand *won* in advance
   pay.
What will we do?
Today's the first day off in a while,
and yet I feel restless.
Can't write a letter, can't pick up a book . . .
So we play chess,
amuse ourselves with *coin betting*
and share some *soju* with dried fish,
while thinking we should do something,
we should go somewhere.

The hiking club, the soccer club,
the *hanja* club, and the book club
all pushed aside by extra work and extra workdays.
No way of making any plans . . .
At this rate, even my love, Jeongsun,
whom I have not seen in three weeks,
might fly away from me.

During education sessions, the boss always says,
free time makes us spend money,
work hard when we're young,
and extra workload and extra workdays are for our own
    good,
because we're like family.
What a prick! He doesn't know shit!
I don't buy things, I don't eat out,
I *start early, end late,* and work on holidays.
Plans are shattered,
and the only thing growing is my debt from advance pay.
How I have waited for my day off . . .
Where will we go?
Nowhere to go.
What will we do?
No money to do anything . . .
Since we can't make plans,
on this dazzling day in May,
we sway, with soju glasses in hand,
drinking our sorrow,
drinking our anger,
drinking the worker's bitter grief.

The Han River

The *Han River* opens its breast
like that of a gaunt mother.
The river's wrinkled breast opens and flows without sound.

The river, our tears,
flows toward the frozen winter,
silently weeping.

Spring is far.
We lament and collapse
from hard work, our chests bruised.
The icy wind rages,
but rising and flowing again, with gritted teeth,
is our love, our unrelenting life.

The river flows.
Carrying filth and disgrace,
the Han River flows fiercely.
Churning the ice sheets,
toward the dark winter,
calling for spring,
yearning for spring,
what opens and flows without sound
is the river, our tears.

Longing

When the warm spring sunlight
hits the factory yard,
the yellow petals of forsythia float away,
dancing above the faces of young workers excited for the
   day off.

Longing softly,
I let go of the small yellow hands,
which take flight on the flowery breeze.
Longing for more longing,
my body trembles
until they fall as teardrops.

Appearing as a mirage,
while the wind blows hard,
my longing begins to soak my heart.
You left weeping from the poverty
that pierced our twenty-five-year-old hearts
like the needle of a sewing machine.
How I ache and long for you . . .

The Bar Wagon

Flowers must be growing from sand.
Or the boss must be pregnant.
They say no extra work on this glorious Saturday.

After cleaning our greasy hands with an *Italian towel*,
changing out of work clothes, and lighting a cigarette,
we are buoyant, like a balloon,
and in the mood to drink,
which leads us to part the curtains of the *bar wagon* behind
    the factory.
We begin divided as Team *Soju* and Team *Makgeolli*,
but we soon unify on the *Toad* by a majority vote.
Brother Kim, glowing about his newborn daughter,
is persuaded to buy a plate of grilled eel.
The newlywed Brother Jeong, in the name of increasing
    his vigor,
is coaxed into buying a dish of sea cucumber.
Brother Mun, who got a raise with a new skills license,
is feeling good and orders two pig's feet.
The spread of dishes gets the liquor to do its magic.

Never lend money to a guy who can't get hard at dawn,
    they say.
Exhausted from extra work,
ours don't even budge at dawn.

So we cackle that our wives' things will get moldy in a week.
Brother Jeong is a newlywed, been married for a month,
and Brother Kim says the wife has a plump bottom, likely to
	bear a son,
only if Brother Jeong follows his method of three thrusts
	from the left
and three thrusts from the right,
followed by nine shallow thrusts and one deep push,
to which we gawk, ponder, giggle.
With each glass that comes around,
we melt into a single body.
Brother Song offers Brother Mun a glass to make up for bad
	feelings.
Brother Seo and Brother Park, from the electrical division,
resolve old misunderstandings.
With Brother Kim's cheering, Brother Noh starts piping
	about his glorious past,
about the days when he fought for Korean independence in
	Manchuria,
while selling dogmeat.
The tall tales get louder, and Brother Gong,
who had worked at Busan's Jagalchi fish market,
says to stop because he's heard them a hundred times
and announces that he will sing so we should clap.
Row across the *Duman River*, around the *Oryuk Islands* . . .
Don't leave me, *Forsythia Girl* . . .
Crossing the *Bakdal Pass* in tears . . .
We bang chopsticks on the kettle lid,
shoulders rocking, butts bouncing.
Rat-a-tat, tat-tat, yeah, fuck yeah!
Yeongja, dear, please bring us another spread of food!

A second round? Head home? How about a go-go joint?
Thrifty Brother Shin sits us down
for a few more bottles, and we are roaring drunk.

That prick in the *labor office*, that asshole in operations,
that snake for a boss . . .
We should pummel the bastards on the labor-management
 committee.
Pent-up anger rushes out.
Brother Mun, red with rage,
says these traitors must be smashed.
Brother Jeong mutters that changes should happen in stages,
beginning with the factory cafeteria.

Brother Kim, who went to a good commerce high school,
now a *greaser* like the rest of us,
is our acting accountant and amends the tab,
which only adds to our bar debt.
We pass around a bowl of cold water
and exit the smoky bar wagon.
Arms over one another's shoulders, we stumble.
Standing together, we piss on the factory wall
and curse at the fate of coming into work on Sunday.
We each finagle a bag of strawberries from a fruit seller for a
 thousand *won*
and stuff it into our coat pockets.
We wave goodbye and hum as we walk,
on this one Saturday evening with no extra work,
heading home, where our sweethearts await.

Garibong Market

As night falls on *Garibong Market,*
beneath the incandescent bulbs hanging over every stall,
the flushed faces of the people, coming and going,
grow warm, heated.

We who had been trapped in lengthy labor
become free flying birds,
going here, stopping there, giggling.
Thugs seeking jobs, uprooted ex-cons,
and bar girls who make a living by pushing their bodies
all get heated with shining eyes.

Whenever I get some money, I first go to Garibong Market,
with good friends, to buy some *tteokbokki,* a dish of *gimbap,*
and a pint of draft beer if I feel like it.
With that I'm as full as a boss who eats steak.
If the colors of a thousand-*won* T-shirt look right,
then friends say my bright face looks glamorous.

Even as we wear ourselves out,
our hands and feet swollen,
working fourteen hours a day,
making brand-name clothes
or assembling expensive audio equipment,
none is for us.

Our hands make them, but they're beyond our reach,
so we throng the Garibong Market
and gaze, dazzled,
at the cheap products made by subcontractors.
I make a promise to treat myself to a blue dress this month.

Myeongji, the front-panel *sida*, says that all she wants
when she gets paid this month is to eat a plate of *Kentucky chicken.*
Jeongi, who puts on the finishing touches, says she saw
some pretty sandals for 2,800 won and waits for a day
 without extra work,
when we can go to the market together.

As the night arrives at Garibong Market,
after sending off the goods,
which we made with our care and blood,
to opulent department stores,
across the sea to a land of big noses,
we, *factory boys* and *factory girls,*
hungry and weary,
set our eyes on the cheap stuff.
Soothing our hunger with a three-hundred-won plate
 of *sundae,*
looking here and looking there,
and after only looking,
feeling despondent,
we turn our steps toward home.

Calling for Fingerprints

We hunch together and
plow our way through the sleet,
and as we enter the *donghoe* building,
we say how good it is
to run errands during work hours.

Peeling the back layer of the photo
of a shabby twenty-nine-year-old self,
I think about the six years buried in the *Garibong Factory
    District.*
Time flows, night and day,
into labor, like meaningless death,
which forces me to confirm that I am still a citizen
who must renew the registration card.

I raise my proud hand, blackened and rough,
with which I feed and support my family
by producing goods for export,
without once committing a crime,
and make a fingerprint.
Ah . . .
Clearly nothing there.
Nothing.
Eaten away by labor,
my fingerprint, which distinguishes me from you,

different for each person, has vanished.
There's nothing left, and it's gone from
Brother Jeong and Brother Lee and Brother Mun, too.
The *attending police* get angry.
During the course of long labor,
our fingerprints, our youth, our existence
have all vanished,
buried in the products sent across the sea.

The women from the chemical goods factory
burst into tears when their fingerprints fail
to emerge after pressing several times.
One after another, all of us without fingerprints
have no existence.
Brother Jeong jokes
that we'll leave no trace as thieves,
but nobody feels like laughing.

We who have no fingerprints
plunge back into the sleet falling like pellets,
and in frozen silence,
we remind ourselves that we are still citizens,
as we bury ourselves again in the factory.
Calling for our fingerprints
to revive clearly . . .
Calling for a worker's renewed life . . .
Calling and calling,
for the revival
of our existence,
the springtime for workers.
Into the sleet we go,
with a burning yearn.

English Conversation

Our mother, widowed early,
died with her pale eyes wide open,
while spraying pesticide over a rice paddy a tenth of an acre.
When I was blindly departing for Seoul,
a bloodletting cry like a cuckoo bird came from behind me,
and the snot-nosed Yeongseok shook off auntie's hand
and held onto my skirt, saying he wants to follow his sister.
He is now a middle school student,
and after reading an English book late into the night,
he says, muttering in his sleep,
that the score on his English listening exam
is lower than the score of kids from well-to-do families
because he doesn't have a cassette player.

Your sister is a *factory girl*
at an American electronics company, a second-line leader,
and I will surely buy that cassette player
for you next month, my Yeongseok,
even if I need to do more overtime,
alert like a sharpened blade,
although my neck is sore
from the *QC activities*.
When I come staggering home at midnight after extra work,
Yeongseok has awkwardly prepared my dinner,
though I had angrily told him not to,

and is practicing English conversation,
his voice clear and rolling.

Your sister couldn't finish school
and is an ignorant factory girl,
but you, Yeongseok, must study hard
and become a really, really great person.
But, dear Yeongseok,
you must not climb on top of people
and make them shed tears of blood.

Whenever you're absorbed in studying English,
I think about our national history
that I learned at the union meeting.
The sons and daughters of the wealthy class
learn English from kindergarten
and attend schools for foreigners.
As a middle school student,
you mutter English in your sleep.
Signboards and brand names
are filled with squiggly writing.
TV and the radio tell us that
only a person polished in English
can be called a sophisticated, educated, and contemporary
    person.
Your ignorant factory girl sister,
a second-line leader at an American electronics company,
can't stop thinking about our country's history,
which I learned at the union meeting.

They took away our speech, script, name, and soul.
They plundered our paddies, fields, grains, products,
and eventually the workers' lives.
The steady plundering of Imperial Japan . . .

I think about the eradication
   of the Korean language.
When I, your sister, the second-line leader at an American
   company, am
pushed to the edge from all the QC work,
scrambling for the parts that surge on the conveyor belt,
I think about the eradication
of the Korean language.

Off to Rot

—For a younger friend leaving for military service

For five years since you entered the factory gates,
with the baby face of a sixteen-year-old,
you have spent nights and days on the machine,
with no proper food, no proper fun,
and nothing to show for it.
You once struggled to accept the sorrowful *grease meal,*
but you have emerged as a man, and now you're leaving for military service,
off to rot during your golden youth.

This no-good older friend
has nothing to give you as you set off
while shedding big tears,
nothing but a farewell glass of bitter *soju.*
But, dear Cheolsu,
you are not really setting off to rot.
Each day of the three years in green uniform
will be a valuable moment you cannot throw away.

Even in the military, you must live diligently.
Don't covet an administrative job or a cozy assignment.
Don't get out of line among your companions.

Even when you face the shameless acts of those who learned
    more and have more,
despite the military life of wearing the same uniform,
eating the same *jjambap* meals, and all sweating the same,
make sure you are recognized
only through sincerity and hard work.

Pick up the broom once more,
clean one more plate,
and work wholeheartedly on all projects.
Push when told to push, pull when told to pull.
Don't look for shortcuts, live with enthusiasm.
The tyranny of seniors or the bullying of higher-ups
may get you down,
and you might suspect that you alone are having a hard time,
but know that you, too, with time, will become a senior.
Isn't the military life of everyone spinning equally
fairer and cleaner than society at large,
where you sell your labor for low wages
and struggle with overtime that keeps increasing?
From within, learn about submission that is beyond servility.
Learn about true labor, where everyone sweats together for
    the common good.

Through practice-oriented love based on action with your
    body,
and through the spirit of sacrifice that does not reject dirty
    jobs,
seek out and make good friends.
In a society where decisions are made through money, school
    cliques, and connections,
coming to realize with your whole being,
together with friends bearing the same painful wounds,
that only sincerity and hard work are true, precious values,
you become unified with others through close cooperation.

Earn the friendship of good people.

Develop courage and take risks amid echoing laughter.
Cultivate tenacity through raids and marches and torment.
Raise your courage to act according to the true meaning of
 a command,
and broaden your capacity to embrace the subordinates.
When time permits, read, think, reflect,
study hard.
During silent guard posts with moonlight pouring down,
ponder the tragedy of national division.

You are setting off, while weeping,
to rot for three years in the military.
Until the day you come back
as a flower bud,
you must rot well.

This no-good older friend,
and you, and our companions,
until the day when we shake the world
as splendid flower buds,
let us rot well together.
Then, as a sturdy worker,
tried and tested,
with good friends
whose lives are steeped in labor, practice, and cooperation,
with your face shining,
come back to us.

Dear Cheolsu, dry your tears.
With a worker's tenacious vitality
you must try hard
to rot well.

Record of My Journey with Men

Early on, when I was a *sida*
I was fond of Jinsu from the inspection team,
not only tall and good-looking but
with eyes and backside lonesome like a deer.
That autumn, we walked together till late night,
but as time went by, my heart turned into a withered leaf.

After becoming a sewing-machine operator,
I desperately wanted to learn,
so I fell in love with the kind college son of my landlord,
and I would read till dawn despite my weary body,
but between us flowed
a deep, unbridgeable river.

After becoming a team leader, I liked Section Head Kim,
who spent money well, nice and stylish,
dignified when giving orders, warmhearted.
I tried smiling at him under the lamp of a western restaurant
but it was pointless, like the froth of a beer.

The winter spent with the manly and wild Jeongyeol,
who could embrace my restless existence,
was painful and rough like a wounded old tree.

Around the time when I became a team leader,
my friends caught the marriage bug.
I felt love for the honest and family-oriented Yeonghun,
but he became exhausted from my selfishness and
 self-righteousness.
He wanted to leave, so I let him go.

Eight years working at the sewing machine,
the company grew big,
from a hundred workers to fifteen hundred,
but all I have left are a rented room with a deposit worth
 half a million *won*,
a cassette player purchased with monthly installments,
and a worn-out twenty-five-year-old body.

A praise from the manager or a get-together with the
 director
would invariably be followed by a demand to increase
 productivity.
I would yell at all sidas,
while running my machine like crazy.
Walking home late at night after overtime,
growing weary from the heaviness,
I say to myself, gritting my teeth,
this can't go on, this isn't it.

After lunch, a wind rises from the cutting team.
They sit on the ground, lean back,
and demand a 50 percent increase in wage,
which had been frozen for two years.
Gukman grabs me,
and, with shining eyes, convinces me
that if we unite, we can win,
that we should not be used anymore.

We walk the factory grounds,
my eyes moist with tears,
and raise all the parched hearts
into a fervid unity.
The battlefield-like factory grounds are momentarily
    wrapped in tense silence,
despite the flustered manager's screams and curses,
and my heart becomes a peaceful land for the very first time,
as fresh shoots of life sprout vigorously.

I had thought that Gukman was delicate, good only at
    joking,
but seeing him with clear determination, engaged in
    practice,
amid the trust of our companions,
with courage more dignified
and conviction more lucid than the company president,
while nurturing great love that is ready for sacrifice,
I find myself filled with warm emotions
during the three days of battle.

Such a man is a genuine man,
a real man with whom I come alive with happiness
as I share my life and give everything I have.
I hold my fast-beating heart
knowing that we shall fight any adversity together.
I calm myself until I am
taut and even like a bowstring.

Incomprehensible Tales

They say exporting is getting more difficult,
and the national debt is the world's third largest.
They say we should reduce consumption and save money.
They say we need to stabilize prices.
Yet when I come home tired after working overtime,
a pretty woman on television
is advertising VCRs, stereos, and air conditioners,
insisting that at least a color TV, a fridge,
and a washing machine are necessary items,
urging me, with an enticing smile,
to eat, dress, and spend with distinction.

During our ten-minute break,
we gather, smoke cigarettes,
and lament about what is happening to our world,
that whatever the case, the workers are hurting more and more.
Really don't know what's what . . .
The country is in a bad state,
yet golf courses built over farmland are full of cars at
    midday,
condominiums sell like hotcakes,
luxury-brand loyalty is on the rise,
and the production of high-class cars can't keep up with demand.
Saunas, massage parlors, and hotels are springing up
    everywhere,

fancy brothel restaurants stay open all night,
and billions are spent on international beauty pageants,
    song festivals, and sporting events.
To ask whether all this is fine is causing only dread.

The newspaper says that prices haven't gone up,
but the landlord is demanding a higher rent.
Utility bills get bigger,
and each time my wife returns from the market,
carrying a lighter bag, she is tearful.
Stunned by the wage-freeze policy,
we work four extra hours a week,
but my wife's despondent sigh grows
on seeing our household account deeper in the red.
Cheers rise at the pro baseball stadium,
excitement swells at the pro soccer stadium,
and we really don't know what's what.

People in high positions from other countries come to
    Korea in streams,
admiring the prosperity and the progress.
They say the national income is increasing,
big companies are expanding,
splendid buildings are going up everywhere,
the '88 Olympics are calling the whole world,
and a welfare society based on justice has been established.
But we are tied down by a wage freeze,
and working hours only increase as the days go by.
Steadying our shaking bodies,
weighed down with fatigue,
we walk the dark byways of prosperity.
    —University students shout for democracy,
    and the company friend next to me whispers
    about the rumors of a democratic labor union—

Becoming Wise

If some guy offers to buy me coffee,
I know he wants something.

If some elegant fellow
pats me on the back with a sweet smile,
I know what he wants from me.

When they bow and seem moved,
with unusual treatment and compliments,
I know they're after something.

When we rise up,
we know that behind the cordial smiles,
behind the mouths repeating "labor and management must
   cooperate," as they retreat,
they're hiding intrigue and daggers.

The educated high-ups are not the only ones who are wise.
Rolling from an early age at the bottom of the world,
getting by amid unending betrayal and defeat,
we learn the ways of life with our *tongbak*.

Above the poor wretches who crawl through the world,
there are folks flying lightly like wizards.
Crawling without wings on the greasy floor,

we live hunched up, rolling around with our instinctive
 heads, our tongbak.
The more we roll our tongbak, however,
the more we unite, our heads coming together,
turning into one enormous tongbak.

Although we haven't learned shit,
with our enormous tongbak,
we know about those whose wings are made of money and
 knives.
We know what kind of place this world has become,
and whom it's for.

Amid bitter tears, crackdowns, and defeat,
as we roll and roll,
our enormous heads colliding and uniting,
our tongbak becomes sharp, precise,
and steady.

As our heads merge to form a single head,
an enormous tongbak,
we'll roll on through this miserable world
toward a new day of the working people.

PART II

Dawn of Labor

Bargain Sale

Today I again roam the industrial area
until crimson twilight covers the Seoul sky.
Looking and roaming,
but nothing, not a single thing.
Alive at twenty-seven,
but no job with which to earn a living.

A single bus token in my pocket.
I soak my heart with a glass of *soju* at a *bar wagon*.
Over the asphalt where rootless laughter flows,
among the shiny streetlights,
I, jobless, walk aimlessly.

After ten years choking on the *grease meal,*
my labor is four thousand *won* a day.
Posted in bright shopwindows are a slew of bargain sale signs.
The subway vendor's voice,
hoarse from hawking clothes for five hundred won apiece,
fades away.
The smile—white as a chestnut flower—guiding my wrist
is also having a 50 percent bargain sale.

Well, fuck . . .
I'll hold my own bargain sale.

I'll take thirty-five hundred won or even three thousand
 won,
as long as I am sold.
Bargain sale! Bargain sale!
But there is one thing.
You'll have to buy my sorrow, my despair,
and my anger, too!

The Dream of an Apprentice

A long night at the factory,
fatigue descends like a cold snap
on aching shoulders.

The machine roaring . . . *Du-ru-ruk* . . . *duk-duk* . . .
Riding the sewing machine, the dreamy sewing machine,
staying awake through the night with two *Taiming* pills . . .
The cold hands of a *sida*
cut away the rosy dreams,
snipping all the impossible, futile dreams
and feeding the blood-flowing leather pieces into the sewing
　　machine,
endlessly feeding.

Still only a sida . . .
I want to mount the sewing machine.
I want to ride that sewing machine
with the dignified face of a warrior.
I want to make clothing
that can envelop and warm the frozen body.
I want to mend this torn household.
The body shivering from the cold,
while cutting, hammering, ironing,
still only a sida . . .
Riding the sewing machine on high,

the dream of a sida
is to connect as one
all that is divided in the world.
The slight body of a sida
sways from the icy winds
blowing through the streets of the factory district.
Above the pale forehead
shines the morning star.

Spring

Once lunchtime comes,
awaited throughout the morning while she rubbed her
 empty stomach,
the spring sunshine is warm even in the corners of the
 factory yard.

Leaning against the still-cold cement wall,
the young workers, their stomachs full, talk copiously.
When she raises her sleepy eyes,
the yearning memory of her hometown quivers
like the waves of rising heat.

How much debt has been paid off with the money
she had sent, the money saved by eating less?
Her mother's wrinkled hands, her father's furrowed,
 sunburned face,
and the faces of her young siblings whining, laughing, and
 quarreling
are clear as azalea petals.

All winter she waited eagerly for spring,
with teeth clenched more bitterly than the bitter cold and
 bitter hardship.
Walking the city streets,
she desires to wear new spring clothes,

and she wants to fill up on tasty treats,
but, biting her lips,
she decides to endure everything gently and sincerely.
Ring...
Suki responds to the bell
announcing the afternoon shift,
the spring breeze lightly lifting her brisk steps.

Sleepiness

When the date for shipment draws near,
a difficult march begins,
raging tirelessly far and wide.
Even if I were told not to do it,
to cover the increased rent,
to catch up on *savings club* payments missed from sickness,
I have to eat seventy-eight hours a week,
even eighty-four hours.

A ghost that couldn't get enough work
or sleep in a previous life
must have entered my body.
Whether I pinch or prod or bite my tongue,
the waves of sleepiness in the ocean of fatigue rush in.
Dozing and nodding . . .
The shiny blade of the *press* comes down and cuts clean.
Sunjeong, who pushes hard on the sewing machine,
is maneuvering like a robot, even as her eyes are closed.
A young *sida*,
who smashed her hand with a hammer,
is crying as her eyes are closing.

From the workshop loudspeakers
flow Michael Jackson's shrills
and Jo Yongpil's crooning, endlessly,

and even if the manager keeps screaming in rage,
drowsiness comes coiling, bottomless and endless.
We wrap bleeding fingers
while wishing
we could become automated machines,
animals that never sleep.

Morning, midday, and nights, too,
without a moment of a clear day,
madly, I'm madly tired.
I am grateful to my two whole hands,
which still keep laboring even in a dream.
My twenty-seven-year-old youthful life,
pickled in fatigue and sleepiness
like dark salted radish.
Still I rise when morning comes, with a bleeding nose,
and dragged by the bonds of low pay,
which is harsher than sleepiness.
In a new morning of prosperity where the sunlight, too, is
    glorious,
I end up kneeling
before a cursed machine,
a hellish battleground,
dozing, hobbling.

Working on Sunday

By the time I hurriedly caught a late bus,
after four hours of extra work,
and groped my way down a dark alley and reached our
    dwelling,
darling little Minju was already a baby star in dreamland.

She hasn't seen her dad's face in a week,
so tonight she swore she would see his face before falling
    asleep,
staying awake by coloring and drawing, my wife says,
    smiling weakly.
She was lulled to sleep with a promise that tomorrow, it
    being Sunday,
she could go somewhere fun with her dad.

Wages did not increase this year, again, yet the landlord
is saying the deposit money needs to go up by five hundred
    thousand *won*.
Then this month is the anniversary ceremony of Mother's
    passing,
and next month Myeongseon's wedding.
Next year we'll have to send little Minju to kindergarten.

So long as none of us falls sick,

so long as we eat only kimchi and rice, and nothing bad
    happens,
so long as I manage to keep working seventy-eight hours
    a week,
so long as we can finish the remaining ten payments for our
    savings club . . .
Since spring, my vertigo has gotten worse.
I feel unstable, as if walking on a tightrope.

On the calendar hanging on the wall,
Minju has used a crayon
to draw a circle around six dates,
saying those are her dad's days off.

Little Minju,
the red dates on that calendar
aren't your dad's days off.
They're holidays for the well-off talented people whose
    bellies are full.
Dear little Minju, sound asleep,
we wish only to raise you well,
and that is why those red dates you are looking forward to
and drew circles around are the days when your dad has
    extra work.
Renouncing the sunny, spring-green Sunday,
your dad will set off with heavy steps and a pale face,
to do extra work.

As a worker in the *fatherland of progress*,
Minju's dad
is snared in the trap of low pay.
That is why on a day marked in red, dear Minju,
your dad is going in to do extra work,
like a hollow and hardened ox.

A Hand Grave

Brother Jeong, who had said,
while smoking an *Eunhasu* cigarette,
that he shall, on Children's Day,
hold his wife and son by the hand
and go to the Grand Children's Park,
got his hand chopped off.

Since he was wearing work clothes,
he couldn't get a ride in
the factory owner's *Granada*,
the factory manager's *Royale Salon*,
or the section head's *Stella*,
so after bleeding for a while,
he went to the hospital in the bed of a *Titan*.

Grabbing the still-twitching hand from the machine
and pulling it out of a greasy glove,
we were lost for words
at the sight of the hand of a thirty-six-year-old grief-filled
    worker.

I put the hand, wrapped in a plastic bag, inside my jacket
and went to Brother Jeong's home
high on *Bongcheondong hilltop*.

Seeing his wife with her gentle eyes and their son's bright
  face,
I could not take out the hand and give it to her.

At a small shop in that shantytown, in broad daylight,
I sat and drank a bottle of *soju*,
then set off to find a book about industrial accidents
that Brother Jeong had asked for.
At the big *Jongno* bookstore, I searched but, dammit,
among the piles of books, I could not find one a worker
  might read.

That fine spring afternoon, on the streets of Jongno,
elegant couples walk in splendid sunshine,
and like the American stores seen in movies,
all sorts of fine things, with foreign brand names, dazzle.
I, with my work boots,
feel nervous like an escaped convict.

Sedans line up in front of tall buildings with luxury saunas.
Cars fill up the space in front of high-class brothels.
Huge department stores are packed.
Clamors rise from the pro baseball stadium.
At an hour when workers, alert like a knife,
are toiling their balls off,
why are there so many guys and gals languidly having fun?
I become an ET
and, like a madman without a soul,
I wander the Jongno streets of our *fatherland of progress*
  —where you can get whatever you want
  and achieve whatever you wish for—
only to go back to being a worker
making four thousand eight hundred *won* a day
and punch my card for extended work.

Brother Jeong's hand that I've kept in my jacket
has grown cold and blue,
so we wash it with soju
and bury it at the base of a sunny factory wall.
We bury
the yellow hands of exploitation
that seek only pleasure in the fatherland of prosperity,
the white hands that eat and play without working,
above the blood and sweat of workers.
With a *press* machine we chop these hands clean
and bury them with tears of rage.
Until the working hands
come back alive, waving with joy,
we bury and bury some more.

Maybe

Maybe I'm a machine, I'm not sure.
As I frantically solder together components
carried along on a conveyor belt,
robotically repeating the same motion thousands of times,
I may have turned into a machine, I'm not sure.

Maybe we're chickens at an egg farm.
Sitting in rows at the production line,
under pale lighting,
moving our hands at the required speed,
laying more eggs if cheerful music is piped in.
We may be chickens at an egg farm.
Once worn-out and no longer laying eggs,
we are turned into *Kentucky chicken*.
We may be chickens at an egg farm.

Slender Jeongsun, seeing no point in going on,
left in tears to work in a beer hall.
Yeongnam, troubled with stomach problems,
became a sick chicken and left for his ruined home village.
Jaesim gritted his teeth and resolutely completed *night school*,
but after failing to get a job as a clerk,
he tore up the graduation certificate and collapsed.
Maybe we are nothing but yoked animals.

Maybe those
who eat the eggs
are really thieves in daylight,
turning people into machines,
    as expendables,
    as commodities,
decent, lawful thieves in daylight.

Maybe the gracious smiles,
the sophisticated beauty and refinement,
the wealthy, glittering splendor,
really belong to us.
Maybe they are just vampires,
standing above our bloody tears, our despair, our pain,
thoroughly sucking out
our laughter and beauty and light.

When I Give You Up

When I gave up the purehearted woman, my first love,
having lost interest, wanting more on the outside,
there beneath the dim streetlight
she did not grab me and said nothing.
She slowly went back to her dormitory, shedding big tears.

By the time I came to understand life better,
the purehearted, sincere woman
had been laid off far ahead of me,
gone to another factory,
and was smiling quietly as she waved
at my stupidity.

The frozen silence after two years of effort . . .
I blamed my sleeping companions, calling them cripples.
I shook my companions lying in despair and defeat,
but they were not moving before the dying sea.
I grew weary in body and spirit.

Losing hope after ten years of trying,
on the morning when I went to work with a resignation
    letter in my pocket,
hoping to sow my seed elsewhere,
my companions, in commotion,
stopped their working hands,

saw eye to eye, and ignited a spark.
Words and hearts became one,
and with a roar, a great wave came crashing.
Twelve hundred sets of muscles surged,
sweeping in like a great tidal wave,
on this day when we stood up.

I could not see,
as I was when I had abandoned her,
so I failed to believe in my brothers.

We are not machines but humans.
We are workers, oppressed and robbed.
We are a mighty deep sea
that could form a tidal wave when we stand up.
While I remained buried,
impatient and rash,
unable to overcome my tedium,
I tried to abandon my brothers.

As the quiet sea
becomes a tidal wave,
with firm belief and righteous practice,
with dogged tenacity,
we shall not hasten,
but neither shall we stop for rest.

A Real Worker

Living this life,
working down to the bone,
obliged to *start early, end late* . . .
But what comes back is only a pittance.

There are folks who produce frantically,
while struggling to live like humans,
as endless metal dust flies up, clogging everything.
And there are folks who play like gods,
with their golf clubs fastened,
welcoming, with patriotic applause, the bulldozer-like
    erection-giving profiteering acts.
Why is this motherfucking life so unfair?

Born as a worker in this land,
anyone who lives without thinking is a corpse,
anyone who does not speak is rotten meat,
anyone who thinks television is trustworthy is a fool,
anyone who talks big has a flawed cock.
A person who acts,
only a worker who moves and practices within life among
    companions,
is a true human,
is a real worker.

Not every snake is a snake.
It takes venom to be a real snake.
Not every lathe is a lathe.
It must be loaded with a *bit* to be a lathe.
Not every worker is a worker.
One must walk shoulder to shoulder with companions,
push away the bulldozer and gather what is ours,
like the blade of an excavator bucket,
in order to be a real worker.

For a Peaceful Evening

My soul has been in anguish,
perhaps from the moment I was born,
or perhaps after I became a worker.

I wake up at dawn,
the day's labor about to begin again.
The merciless spinning of huge machines,
and the boss's cold expression,
sweep over me like darkness.
If I ever kill myself,
I'll probably do it at dawn.

Going home late, after working extra hours,
the deep anguish of being alive, of living as a worker,
once again overtakes me.

On a bright Sunday,
amid the laughter from a peaceful family meal,
the thought of tomorrow's lack of guarantees
overwhelms me with dark anxiety.

Since being born into this world,
I have committed no crime,
and I am neither slave nor serf.
I live and work honorably, productively

in the Republic of Korea, a land of stability and prosperity,
where plentiful laughter makes the heavens ring,
so why is my life plagued by the anxiety of a servant?

All I have are my own body,
my sweet wife, my lovely daughter,
and a one-room home on lease.
The long agonizing work . . .
No matter how much I save,
spending nothing on food and clothes,
little remains, like bubbles.
At this rate I might collapse one day.

Is there no hope of awaking fresh in the morning,
sweating joyfully at my work,
and then, as the sun is setting,
after laughing together with companions as we leave the
    factory,
spending a peaceful evening at home,
sharing a simple meal?

Who is trampling on our dream
of working honorably
and enjoying a peaceful evening at home?
What is making us restless?
After living restlessly for thirty years,
the time has come,
for the sake of a peaceful evening,
for the sake of a peaceful future,
to set off on the workers' inevitable road,
where no peace will be found.
Right through the middle of uncertainty,
resolutely, resolutely,
we shall advance.

Dawn of Labor

The warlike night labor once over,
I pour cold *soju*
over my aching heart.
Ah . . .
I can't go on like this for long.
For sure, I can't go on like this.

A life of badly cooked factory meals of *jjambap* . . .
My body covered in grease, in a trial of strength,
I flounder and squeeze everything out
in this war of labor.
Although I can't go on for long,
although I can't go on for sure,
there is no other way.

If only I could get free,
if only I could fly out from
my depleted shadowy fate at twenty-nine . . .
But, alas,
there is no other way, no other way.
Apart from death, there is no other way.
This dogged life,
the yoke of poverty,
there is no other way but to live this fate.

Into my slumping body,
for the sake of tomorrow's work, which always comes,
I pour cold soju, at dawn,
onto my aching heart.
I also pour tenacity, dignity, fury, and sorrow,
which are stronger than soju.

Inside each raw drop of sweat and blood,
which will, in the end, break and erupt
from the helpless wall of despair,
there grows, with calm breath,
our love, our fury,
our hope and unity.
For that, at dawn, we pour cold soju
onto our aching hearts,
again and again,
until a new dawn for workers
comes arising.

No Other Way

Three factory meals of badly cooked rice that have
    no glaze
and this everyday labor, which melts my bones,
are making me ill,
my legs getting shaky as I grow older,
but there is no other way.

Although I crouch in the freezing courtyard,
poisoned by the gas from burning briquettes,
for the third time this winter,
there is no other way but to live my life in this small, rented
    room.

Although I grow deaf from the noise on the factory floor
and my lungs gurgle from the inhaled cloud of dust,
there is no other way.

With the death of Brother Kim,
the eleventh victim of work accidents,
who used to delight us with Jo Yongpil songs
as we shared *soju* and *ramyeon*,
we said to ourselves,
it's time to leave,
but in this career, there is no other way.

Indeed, there is no other way.
Although we fall sick, lose a hand, even die,
for the sake of our unrelenting life,
there is no other way but this poverty, this everyday labor.

Living is
working till we drop, sleeping sparsely,
washing greasy clothes, shivering in rented hovels,
and shrinking in anxiety and grief.
Still, there is no other way.

People high as the heavens climb higher like gods,
while we grow ever smaller,
but there is no other way.

Yet, for us to live as humans,
there is no other way
but to unite the surging waves
and overturn the world in a flash.
Arriving like a storm,
in quest of what is ours,
we take a colossal step forward, in outcry,
because there is no other way.
There is no other way.

Sunset

The sun setting behind those hills
stretches out a hand through dull windows,
making the sewing machine needles sparkle.
Rubbing my eyes in the shimmer,
remembering the production goals,
I push hard on the pedal as sweat runs down my back.

Today, setting aside the dirty laundry, accumulated
    fatigue,
and even the *hanja* study,
I wanted to meet a friend from my hometown,
who had been waiting to get in touch,
and hear the news of my parents, of home.
Intent on unburdening myself, I worked feverishly,
but I was told
    —If you're not about to collapse,
  then stop the nonsense and do extra work—
At the boss's shout,
the sunset glows crimson.

The team leader's exasperation
has forced me to sign up to do extra work,
while the *sida* Myeongji, sick since the morning
and overwhelmed by the workload, is tearful.
Through the noise of sewing machines and hammers,

the radio speakers are blasting
   —After a rewarding day's work, while enjoying a cozy
     moment of rest,
a peaceful cup of coffee,
and a chat with someone you love,
this evening the sunset is beautiful,
the mountain breeze fresh.
Let's take in the news of celebrities, followed by the latest
   in pro baseball
and more great pop music. First, here's a song by Jeong
   Sura . . .
"Ah, Ah . . . Our Republic of Korea"—
My study of hanja, for which I had resolved,
with my teeth clenched,
to write a page each day before sleeping, no matter how
   tired I felt,
petered out a few days ago.
A novel I received as a birthday present is still unread after
   a month.
It has been a long time since I wrote a letter home.
I can't count the number of plans
that have collapsed, been revived, and collapsed again.
With a fading sigh, frustrated and angry,
wondering what the point is of living,
du-ruk du-ru-ruk duk-duk,
I step on the pedal.

As the setting sun
emits its last dark crimson glow,
Suni's sorrow and Myeongji's tears
and Jeongja's fury are swallowed up
by the growing darkness.
Indeed so, from darkness to darkness,
despairing in endless labor,
standing up again when we collapse,

pouring sorrowful tears as oil to burn,
we hold one another's hands.
Let's never let go of love and hope,
the cozy rest and peace offered by the glow of sunset,
which we shall hold in our breast,
until we gain our rights.
In the darkness of sorrow and despair,
let's never let go
of one another's hands.

PART III

For a New Land

Love

Love is
sorrow, heartrending grief.
Love is fury, utter hatred.
Love is wailing, writhing, covered in blood.
Love is separation,
a clear separation toward unity.
Love is pain, dreadful pain.
Love is action, concrete action.
Love is labor, the dull, aching path of the worker.
Love is taking oneself apart,
melting into history, and being reborn as multitude.
Love is cruel, a cold decision.
Love is struggle, merciless struggle.
Love is a maelstrom,
the oceans, mountains, fields, and the sky awaking,
storm and lightning thrashing and roaring,
being reborn the color of blood.
In the end, love is
a peaceful shining sea,
a blue sky with sunlight pouring down,
all living things becoming one
on verdant, dew-soaked land,
a dazzling new day filled with song and dance,
a wondrous conception.

The Wind to the Stones

The flowers planted in sand
do not bloom even on sunny spring days.
Bamboos clamor together
due to the blowing wind.
Reeds hold up their hands and howl
because of the raging wind.
Stones roll and start a landslide
because they cannot bear their weight against the wind.

Bamboos, reeds, stones
roar because the wind blows.

We want to lead quiet lives.
We know well that what will come back to us
are only disgraced layoffs and hunger,
a taste of the club, and life behind bars,
so who would dare to roar and stand up?
You blame us for causing labor problems,
yet we want to live quietly like stones, like grass.
But the dry roots planted in sand
must spread toward the fertile soil.
We, too, want to bear flowers and fragrance on spring days.
What makes us roar and create landslides
is the wind raging madly,
which we can no longer endure.

Searching for Food

This kind of food?
Couldn't feed it to a rich man's dog.
Even machines would thump and rattle.
We refused to eat,
then gathered on the roof,
our last refuge.

The wind was cold, eager to freeze our hearts,
which had opened slightly and begun to burn.
Shoulder to shoulder, sharing one another's warmth,
all we could enjoy was the freedom to starve.
We filled our stomachs with laughter like falling leaves.

When we stood up like bamboo shoots,
with our rough faces trembling
and the sound of their shoes imposing,
their glossy faces pressed down heavily.
As our frightened eyes met,
we saw ourselves resolute
like sunlight pushing away the dark clouds.

Who will shake us, as firm as a rock,
entangled more tightly
than the gear wheels that ate our fingers?

Who will separate us as we search for our way to live,
    our *bap*?

The boss said he would treat us like family.
But why are you starving us skinny!
Even an ox needs fodder before it can plow!
How can we work on food like this?
Yeongju, who coughs up blood nightly,
after three years with the *polishing team,* is howling.
Someone shouts,
Your abundant health comes from our rotting bodies!
Your happy laughter is the fruit of our twisted frustration
    and sorrow!
Oh, you!
We'll no longer let ourselves be fooled by your slick tongues.
We won't stay quiet, even if you threaten to call the cops.
Even if you say ignorant *factory girls* and *factory boys* are
    wrecking the business
and threaten to have us arrested,
we'll not back off any longer.

When their faithful dogs raised their clubs,
and our friends ended up covered in blood,
the color of red soaked our hearts and melted away our
    feebleness.
Flames leapt out of our eyes.
Sixteen-year-old Myeongi cried in fear,
her thin body held in my gaunt embrace.
We burned employee awards and company recognitions
and stood up.
We stood up tall,
with the pride of workers who labor and produce all night,
as honorable workers before heaven.
In quest of our bap,
we kicked down the thick wall

with the feet of workers who can no longer retreat.
In quest of bap,
in quest of what belong to us,
fighting with dignity
as five hundred roaring voices echo in the sky above the factory,
we know the deceit behind those smiles,
those concealed claws,
as they plea like innocent lambs.

The abundant bap fills the heart,
as our tears flow again,
as we pass around the *soju* glass.
Now we start!
While we firmly held hands
and looked into one another's blazing eyes,
there, beyond the frozen ground
swept by blizzards,
a warm spring day
was opening, heavily, painfully.

Confrontation

In the snug office of the company president,
they pounded on the desk,
telling us to abandon the union,
calling us sons of bitches, impure elements.
Their heads, hopping mad,
might be well armed with class ideology
that says owners and workers, like deer and pigs,
can never be equal.

They probably think that working in silence,
doing as we are told,
accepting what we are given, being grateful
for such blessings
in obedience and faithfulness is the only way
for excellent workers to ensure industrial peace and societal stability.
But we know from experience
that there is stability
when human beings respect one another fairly in agreement,
that there is great strength
when we support one another democratically and equally.

This tense confrontation . . .
Feudalistic and authoritarian,

they believe in money and force and power as the almighty
   god.
Unified democratically,
we believe that the world's relations should be based on
   equality and love.

Those with class ideology fixed in their heads
may prefer to separate the wealthy and the workers
as two distinct species like deer and pigs,
but the more they trample on us and crush us,
the more mightily we rise
as humans,
by equality
by democracy
by unity.
What is to be done
about this inevitable confrontation
that is manifesting
and becoming hotter by the day?

A Song about Leaving

Hey-ho,
off I go,
carrying a heart like a coffin.

The coffin covered with white flowers
is heavy with sorrow, with the screams of cut-off fingers,
with lungs eaten away by worms,
with souls whose bloodstains have not dried.
Onward and onward, hey-ho,
off I go.

My friends who hang on with hollow eyes,
don't weep for me because I'm leaving.
Although the place where we met
was the corner of the factory thick with oily dust,
a land of despair,
where we tumbled in agony like raindrops,
the place where we shall meet
is not a place like that.

What we shared
were a few cigarettes and a night's anger tamed by glasses
    of *soju*,
what we shall share is not only that.

When bitter cigarette smoke rose
over our drooping bodies,
remember how we used to envy the birds in the sky.

I'm not setting off like a bird
in search of a cozy nest.

No. I'm a bird holding a bomb
and diving into that immense chimney
spouting the smoke of death.

Hey-ho,
off I go, carrying a heart like a coffin.
Hey-ho,
let us meet again.
Let us meet again in battle,
where crushed bodies and
broken things find their original shape,
for a new land,
full of love, without high and low.

The coffin covered in white flowers
is heavy,
so off I go,
slowly, weeping, limping.
Hey-ho.

Am I Drifting?

I'm not a migratory bird, nor a drifting cloud,
but when I was young,
searching for my own way of finding food,
as my tears fell on the yellow dirt roads of my hometown,
I left for Seoul.

About the time my ears grew used to the sound of clattering metal,
the cost of three meal tickets a day and the tab at the company store
left me with a pittance for a paycheck,
pushing me out the door.
When I began to feel attached to a place,
a letter of dismissal would shove me in the back,
so I moved from factory to factory.

I intend to settle at a place,
even as the choking *grease meal* is the same as elsewhere.
Why do many things drive me off or give me the boot?
Now I'm sick of wandering the wide streets like a criminal,
with only a suitcase of clothes and a bundle of bedding.
I shudder
at the thought of unfamiliar faces and another shabby treatment,
but must I leave again?

Smiling moon-shaped faces as I lift my eyes . . .
I dream of a workplace where I'm treated like a human,
where I am rewarded as much as I deserve,
as I work hard with the machine comfortable in my hands.
Ah, I can't leave now,
I can't go drifting any longer.
The past I have lived,
uprooted and pushed in all directions,
has left me only lasting wounds,
only nights of sorrowful tears,
only this wrecked body.

I can no longer sit slumped over a dismissal notice
kicking me out.
I'm not a migratory bird, nor a drifting cloud.
Now it's time to put down roots,
stand on my feet in my place.
Facing up to them firmly,
searching for the right place for me to be,
I will never let go
of these hands that I clasp tightly,
rough and frail,
warm and strong,
never to be flung away again.

Samcheong Reeducation Camp I

Leaving the still-dark Seoul,
where frost needles stand straight,
the tarp-covered army truck moves north.
With fearful eyes and stifled breaths,
I see the *Three-Eight Bridge*,
supine and gaunt.
Will we come back alive?
Will we cross the Three-Eight Bridge again while alive?
Trembling at the shout of orders and the kicking of boots,
stripped bare and head shaven,
wearing a guerilla uniform and *Tongil Boots*,
rolling left and right over the frozen ground,
I become number 5-134 of the second intake at the
    Samcheong Reeducation Camp.

Bloodshot fury and loyalty and compassion
all smashed by army boots and rifle butts,
without a single smile, I am unable to handle myself.
Broken digits from crawling on the ground with fingers
    locked . . .
Feet frostbitten from minus-twenty-degree ground, flowing
    with pus . . .
Every joint aching from being pummeled,
we crawl to the latrine and excrete dark bloody shit,
where we whimper quietly for the first time,

until we leap to our feet at the sound of the whistle to
    assemble.

Crawling the drill ground in a snowstorm,
then on to the *Wonsan bombing stance,* the frog jumping,
    PT calisthenics . . .
Sent back to the start if we fall behind,
stamped on if we collapse,
bloodied with a wooden beam if we squirm.
Then in the barracks, forced to do
the *Han River human bridge,* the *grenade-on-the-bed,*
the *helmet roll* . . .
Shins bashed in with army boots,
punched and kicked against the wall of the *pechka stove,*
frothing at the mouth, sinking . . .
Is this a detention camp or a living hell?

Awakened by a dream of being chewed up by the teeth of
    tank wheels,
chilled sweat running, deliriously moaning and sobbing,
the teeth grinding curses . . .
Still, wishing to check that we are alive,
every night we cautiously open our hearts.

Brother Kim shook his boss's lapels during a strike
    demanding unpaid wages,
so he was reported and brought here.
Fifteen-year-old Song went out at night
to meet his mother returning home from working at a
    construction site
and was dragged in as a hooligan.
A guy was detained for unpaid *ttallabit* to a moneylender,
another one arrested for quarreling at a market.
One person yelled after a drink and was brought in,
another arrested for having danced with a high official's wife.

Amid the fatigue and the pain,
within the maddening loneliness and fear,
we hold one another's frozen, chapped hands weakly,
telling one another that we must survive
and get out alive.

As the days pass, we turn into wild animals.
Panting and exhausted,
on the edge of the final precipice,
those who begin to stand up and scream,
wishing rather for sweet death,
longing for the warm smell of soft flesh,
demanding to be treated as humans for at least a moment,
get carted off to the dispensary after merciless beatings.
Dying one by one
from ruptured intestines, concussions, and suffocation,
turned into a box of ashes worth three million six hundred
    thousand *won*,
thrown at the feet of a haggard woman with an aching
    heart,
in front of a starry-eyed child
waiting for a dad who had left to make a lot of money.

Brother Lee, dragged here like a dog,
seen as an impure element
for joining the struggle for a democratic labor union,
limping on a grossly swollen leg,
got hacked by a trench shovel and fell dead,
while caring for Old Man Mun,
who was sick and around the age of Brother Lee's father.
Brother Kim, a steelworker, who stood up and said they were
    going too far,
left in an ambulance, head smashed in with a rifle butt.
Brother Sim, detained after extra work for a tattoo on his
    arm,

who boasted about his fiancée, with whom he lived together,
her anxiously waiting eyes always on his mind,
who constantly insisted, on the verge of tears, that he had to
   get out alive,
became icy cold in the end.
Old Man Song, nearly sixty, beaten by soldiers young
   enough to be his grandkids,
who used to say that Imperial Japan's conscription had not
   been as bad as this,
trembled in rage as he went limp.
While Brother Choe, just turned forty, who protested loudly
that he had committed no crime but was brought here only
   because he's an ex-con,
deserted the camp and climbed the White Bone Peak,
where he fought off the encircling soldiers,
until he was blown apart in a furious explosion.

How we thrashed and tried to shake off the nightmare,
every part of our bodies trembling,
to bury and forget the haunting *winter of '80.*
The pallid unforgiving souls who died like dogs,
where on this land are they wandering still?
The poor broods and women left behind,
where on these dazzling streets, driven away as peddlers,
are they bearing the bitterness ghastlier than the neon signs?
The many campmates,
kneading their aching bones on cloudy days,
where, among the hovels of labor,
are they rotting away?
Where are they sharpening their knife blades?

More than the empty scars left by the toes severed from
   frostbite,
more than my aching body,
almost a scrap after those all-night drills,

what needs to be purified
from the torturous days of the past,
truly, indeed truly,
is not us, but them.
In the bloody land of violence,
the dark
blue
hatred
that remains deep
is becoming clear
through splendid light,
reviving
the unforgiving rage of the weak.
Trembling at the memory of
   that winter of '80,
      Samcheong Reeducation Camp.

Mother

Under the blazing sun of meager May and June,
on the island of Namdo,
as you crawled the furrows of the field clutching a hoe,
I suckled at your shriveled breasts.
Taking in the soft and rich food,
the meat and rice that ought to have gone into your body,
I grew up by draining my mother's body like a spider.

I was raised on gruel of foxtail grass,
which often made me dizzy,
then I thrashed as a worker full of grief for having had no
    schooling,
but I never turned to stealing.
I never caused people harm,
never lived idly.
If there is one person in this world
to whom I brought sorrow,
it was you, Mother.

Your one wish in life
was to have a peaceful family,
even if we had few possessions.
I worked hard, made fair demands,
fought with good conscience for our better days.
As the struggle deepened and hardship raged more fiercely,

you grew more apprehensive,
sinking into greater resignation,
embracing, pleading, and reproaching.
Mother!
You are over sixty but still work as a housekeeper.
Your desire is the dream of all of us.
Because we are poor and had no schooling,
because we have dark grief from humiliation and scorn,
your desire for a peaceful family
is indeed an earnest prayer by us all.

Oh, Mother!
Within you is our enemy.
Those who cruelly trample on your desire and hope
for a peaceful family life
lurk cunningly inside your prayers,
like a poisonous snake,
of subservience and selfishness,
of greed and indolence,
and with the steady, persistent tongue of a vicious enemy,
they burrow into our weakest humanity to tempt us.

Born into this world, I drive a nail into your heart,
the heart of the only person I call Mother.
For the sake of your earnest wish,
for the prayers of all mothers on this land,
to regain the happiness that has been stolen and smeared,
today we become wayward children
and set off to the battleground in tears,
leaving your side.

Embracing your tears of blood as well as grief,
we promise to replace them with love and pious affection.
Bloodied in battles to attain our precious peace,
the flags of victory will flutter on high,

and we shall come home with shining faces
and meet you with our heads to the ground.
But until that day, Mother, we are the most wayward
   children under heaven.

To cut out the enemy's tongue lurking inside you,
to sever with cold hostility,
with true love for you, Mother,
we become the most wayward and awful children under
   heaven,
and head out for the battleground shedding tears of blood.
Mother . . .
Mother . . .

A Beautiful Confession

People say I've screwed up my life.
My companions are worried about me.

Look,
there's no life that I've screwed up.
I'm not a captain degraded to a private,
I'm not a bankrupt billionaire,
I've not been fired from public service,
I've not been demoted from director to manager.

After all, the twelve years of skills are alive in my body,
and who cares if I feel a little discomfort, as I felt in my
    many lowly jobs?
With no schooling to start with, and possessing nothing,
    I became a *greaser*.
If I were to crawl madly for a century,
would I become a company president?
Would I become a government minister?
Would I succeed as an office worker?
Three, four months in the cell might even fatten me up,
bring some comfort, and allow me to study.
When was a worker ever special?
I don't have a life to screw up,
and no big deal if I'm branded.

My friends,
don't worry too much.
Am I not living diligently and proudly?
I confess in earnest, in shame.
I was a selfish, arrogant, competitive person.
I called you my friend if you benefitted me,
pushed you away if not.
I distrusted my companions, getting to know them only
    when necessary,
and calculated their use value.
In dejection and falsehood, I merely worked, ate, slept, and
    got drunk
without any meaning to life.
Seeking only style and pleasure, I had a hard time looking
    after myself.

Once I joined the labor movement,
I came to know what a true human life is,
amid the deep trust, sharing, and love from my companions.
What greater thrill than to be recognized for my existence
and to live for my companions in trust and love?
Sharing a bowl of *ramyeon* and a bottle of bitter *soju* is
    enough for joyful laughter.
Free of anxiety and boundaries, you and I together as one,
within shining open unity,
I savor the happiness of emancipation.
If my tears can turn into my companions' laughter,
my suffering into my companions' joy,
my pain into our hope,
what a beautiful, meaningful life this is.

It's okay if people say I've screwed up my life.
Within the fervent setting of the labor movement,
smiles spread across the faces of working sisters and brothers
    of this land,

    the deathly structure of low pay and long hours gets
        smashed.
As a worthy and proud worker,
once again, today, at an unfamiliar workplace,
tedium and indignity gradually fade away,
and tireless flames of struggle burn bright.

I Am Nothing Special

My face is nothing to look at,
and I am poor at speaking.
I have no money and nobody to count on.
I dropped out of school, and I'm not sophisticated.
When I think of my lot,
I am truly a pathetic nobody,
but I never swindle.
I do not rob or crush people,
and I do not cause sorrow to others.

I am nothing special,
but younger friends consider me as kind,
my companions think of me as trustworthy,
and older friends recognize me as well-mannered.

I may be nothing special,
but without me
my good friends who live upright
while fighting for our rights
might have floundered while fending for themselves
and faded away without meaning, like a shooting star.

Sure,
you and I, all of us, are nothing special,
but we are a hardening cement

that gathers the scattered pebbles
and binds them firmly together.

We are not big names with brilliant personalities
with money, backers, and theories,
but we are a stout rope that does not rot,
binding all of us together in firm unity.

We are the workers,
alive and active
at the workplace fighting until the end,
as precious hope within ourselves.

Walls

When I was a tame worker,
exhausted from working long hours,
I lived in the shadow of low wages,
knowing it as the dark wall of my fate.

When I opened my eyes,
a ray of light shone
through the high and thick wall.

When I cried out,
my lips became sealed,
and the only echo returning was a pointless wound.

When I ran and struck it,
the wall did not yield,
and my companions coldly wiped away my blood.

I whispered,
limping and muttering for a long while.
Together, my companions and I entwined,
we struck the wall repeatedly with bare bodies
until the blood-soaked wall began to crack.

We pierced a hole with hammers
and held our breath through the long night as we ignited
    dynamite.
When the enormous wall came crashing down,
the walls in our hearts separating you and me
came crashing down, too.

As we ran up the wide-open hill,
from beneath each dark wall
came the sounds of banging and thumping,
the sounds of encircling and piercing,
and the sounds of terrible screaming.
We set up battle lines again,
with a countless number of comrades,
standing on robust solidarity,
toward our green land of equality
that we deserve to live in.
You are the hammer.
I am the dynamite.
By means of bodies, sparks, bulldozers,
we take a step forward in the workers' progress
that is at once heavy, powerful, precise, and certain.

Until the low wages and long hours,
which had been our fate, vanish . . .
Until the walls of oppression and exploitation
and division vanish . . .

Illusions

If tomorrow morning's newspaper
says that the National Assembly has been abolished,
we would not be surprised.

If it says that the *Union Federation* has been dissolved,
we would no longer be sad.

We shall no longer grieve at court rulings
ordering a crackdown on our efforts to find *bap*.

Even if educated people talk nonsense,
even if monks, priests, and pastors spew drivel,
even if the media betrays us,
we shall not be angry.

We shall no longer rely on or believe these illusions,
these sweet wrappings
that betray our sad love,
our trembling hopes, our wishes.

We shall not be satisfied with the things
they showed us to appease us.
We shall no longer neglect
the things we must rightly find,

which we bitterly realized from
deathly labor and life,
from bloody battles.
We shall no longer be fooled with the illusion
that this fine land
belongs to them.

For our land of the workers,
    for our tomorrow
    by our dreams,
the whole world becoming one, hand in hand,
for a breathtaking new day,
we shall go forward
while smashing the sweet illusions
blocking our path.

노동의 새벽

저임금과 장시간 노동의 암울한 생활 속에서도
희망과 웃음을 잃지 않고
열심히 살며 활동하는 노동 형제들에게
조촐한 술 한 상으로 바칩니다.

1984년 타오르는 5월에
박노해

하늘

우리 세 식구의 밥줄을 쥐고 있는 사장님은
나의 하늘이다

프레스에 찍힌 손을 부여안고 병원으로 갔을 때
손을 붙일 수도 병신을 만들 수도 있는 의사 선생님은
나의 하늘이다

두 달째 임금이 막히고
노조를 결성하다 경찰서에 끌려가
세상에 죄 한번 짓지 않은 우리를
감옥소에 집어넣는다는 경찰관님은
항시 두려운 하늘이다

죄인을 만들 수도 살릴 수도 있는 판검사님은
무서운 하늘이다

관청에 앉아서 흥하게도 망하게도 할 수 있는
관리들은
겁나는 하늘이다

높은 사람, 힘 있는 사람, 돈 많은 사람은
모두 하늘처럼 뵌다
아니, 우리의 생을 관장하는
검은 하늘이시다

나는 어디에서
누구에게 하늘이 되나
대대로 바닥으로만 살아온 힘없는 내가
그 사람에게만은
이제 막 아장걸음마 시작하는
미치게 예쁜 우리 아가에게만은
흔들리는 작은 하늘이것지

아 우리도 하늘이 되고 싶다
짓누르는 먹구름 하늘이 아닌
서로를 받쳐 주는
우리 모두 서로가 서로에게 푸른 하늘이 되는
그런 세상이고 싶다

멈출 수 없지

빨리빨리
바빠 아침을 지어먹고
만원버스 따라 뛰며
종종종 바쁘게 걸어
후다닥 작업복 갈아입고
쓰왜앵 ──
열나게 하루를 돈다

긴 식사대열
식반을 받쳐 들고
국에 말아 훌 마시고
화장실 가서 찌익 오줌 누고 뭐 볼 틈도 없이
뻑뻑 담배 한 대 굽고
연장노동 들어가면
전쟁터처럼 정신없이
굉음 속에 기계는 돌아가고
스피커 악악거리는
박자 빠른 디스코를
따라잡기엔 지쳐 버렸다

땀에 절어 맥 풀린 얼굴들로
종종걸음치며 공장문을 쏟아져 나와
인사조차 못 나눈 채
검은 어둠 속으로 흩어지고
비탈진 골목길을 숨 가쁘게 오르며
나는 때리면 돌아가는 팽이라고
거대한 탈수기에 넣어져 돌리면
돌릴수록 쥐어짜지는 빨래라고
하루, 일 년, 죽을 때까지
정신없이 따라 돌며
정신없이 바뀌는 세상에
눈빛도 미소도 생각조차
속도 속에 빼앗겨 버렸어

전력을 다 짜내어 뛰어도
갈수록 멀어져만 가는
황새를 뱁새걸음으로,
공작새를 장닭으로,
승용차를 맨발로 따라 뛰며

죽기까지 손발을 멈출 수 없지
걷고 싶어도 주저앉고 싶어도
채찍보다 더 무서운
살아야 한다는 것,
노동자의 운명은
죽음이 아니라면 멈출 수 없지

오늘도 내일도
가면 갈수록 바쁘게 뛰어야 하는
갈수록 가진 것 없고 졸라매야 하는
고도로, 번영으로
급성장하는
우리는 복지국가 대한민국
뺑이치는
노동자

신혼일기

길고 긴 일주일의 노동 끝에
언 가슴 웅크리며
찬 새벽길 더듬어
방 안을 들어서면
아내는 벌써 공장 나가고 없다

지난 일주일의 노동,
기인 이별에 한숨 지며
쓴 담배연기 어지러이 내어 뿜으며
바삐 팽개쳐진 아내의 잠옷을 집어 들면
혼자서 밤들을 지낸 외로운 아내 내음에
눈물이 난다

깊은 잠 속에 떨어져 주체못할 피로에 아프게 눈을 뜨면
야간일 끝내고 온 파랗게 언 아내는
가슴 위에 엎으려져 하염없이 쓰다듬고
사랑의 입맞춤에
내 몸은 서서히 생기를 띤다

밥상을 마주하고
지난 일주일의 밀린 얘기에
소곤소곤 정겨운
우리의 하룻밤이 너무도 짧다

날이 밝으면 또다시 이별인데,
괴로운 노동 속으로 기계 되어 돌아가는
우리의 아침이 두려웁다

서로의 사랑으로 희망을 품고 돌아서서
일치 속에서 함께 앞을 보는
가난한 우리의 사랑, 우리의 신혼행진곡

천생연분

내가 당신을 사랑하는 것은
당신이 이뻐서가 아니다
젖은 손이 애처로와서가 아니다
이쁜 걸로야 TV 탈랜트 따를 수 없고
세련미로야 종로거리 여자들 견줄 수 없고
고상하고 귀티 나는 지성미로야
여대생년들 쳐다볼 수도 없겠지
잠자리에서 끝내주는 것은
588 여성동지 발뒤꿈치도 안 차고
써비스로야 식모보단 못하지
음식솜씨 꽃꽂이야 학원강사 따르것나
그래도 나는 당신이 오지게 좋다
살아 볼수록 이 세상에서 당신이 최고이고
겁나게 겁나게 좋드라

내가 동료들과 술망태가 되어 와도
며칠씩 자정 넘어 동료 집을 전전해도
건강 걱정 일 격려에 다시 기운이 솟고
결혼 후 3년 넘게 그 흔한 쎄일샤쓰 하나 못 사도

짜장면 외식 한번 못하고 로숀 하나로 1년 넘게 써도
항상 새순처럼 웃는 당신이 좋소

토요일이면 당신이 무데기로 동료들을 몰고 와
피곤해 지친 나는 주방장이 되어도
요즘 들어 빨래, 연탄갈이, 김치까지
내 몫이 되어도
나는 당신만 있으면 째지게 좋소

조금만 나태하거나 불성실하면
가차 없이 비판하는 진짜 겁나는 당신
좌절하고 지치면 따스한 포옹으로
생명력을 일깨 세우는 당신
나는 쬐끄만 당신 몸 어디에서
그 큰 사랑이, 끝없는 생명력이 나오는가
곤히 잠든 당신 가슴을 열어 보다 멍청하게 웃는다

못 배우고 멍든 공순이와 공돌이로
슬픔과 절망의 밑바닥을 일어서 만난

당신과 나는 천생연분
저임금과 장시간 노동과 억압 속에 시들은
빛나는 대한민국 노동자의 숙명을
당신과 나는 사랑으로 까부수고
밤하늘 별처럼
흐르는 시내처럼
들의 꽃처럼
소곤소곤 평화롭게 살아갈 날을 위하여
우린 결말도 못 보고 눈감을지 몰라
저 거친 발굽 아래
무섭게 소용돌이쳐 오는 탁류 속에
비명조차 못 지르고 휩쓸려갈지도 몰라
그래도 우린 기쁨으로 산다 이 길을
그래도 나는 당신이 눈물 나게 좋다 여보야

도중에 깨진다 해도
우리 속에 살아나
죽음의 역사를 넘어서서
이른 봄마다 당신은 개나리 나는 진달래로

삼천리 방방곡곡 흐드러지게 피어나
봄바람에 입 맞추며 옛 얘기 나누며
일찍이 일 끝내고 쌍쌍이 산에 와서
진달래 개나리 꺾어 물고 푸성귀 같은 웃음 터뜨리는
젊은 노동자들의 모습을 보며
그윽한 눈물로 지자 여보야
나는 당신이 좋다
듬직한 동지며 연인인 당신을
이 세상에서 젤 사랑한다
나는 당신이 미치게 좋다

이불을 꿰매면서

이불홑청을 꿰매면서
속옷 빨래를 하면서
나는 부끄러움의 가슴을 친다

똑같이 공장에서 돌아와 자정이 넘도록
설거지에 방 청소에 고추장 단지 뚜껑까지
마무리하는 아내에게
나는 그저 밥 달라 물 달라 옷 달라 시켰었다

동료들과 노조 일을 하고부터
거만하고 전제적인 기업주의 짓거리가
대접받는 남편의 이름으로
아내에게 자행되고 있음을 아프게 직시한다

명령하는 남자, 순종하는 여자라고
세상이 가르쳐 준 대로
아내를 야금야금 갉아먹으면서
나는 성실한 모범근로자였었다

노조를 만들면서
저들의 칭찬과 모범표창이
고양이 꼬리에 매단 방울 소리임을,
근로자를 가족처럼 사랑하는 보살핌이
허울 좋은 솜사탕임을 똑똑히 깨달았다

편리한 이론과 절대적 권위와 상식으로 포장된
몸서리쳐지는 이윤추구처럼
나 역시 아내를 착취하고
가정의 독재자가 되었었다

투쟁이 깊어 갈수록 실천 속에서
나는 저들의 찌꺼기를 배설해 낸다
노동자는 이윤 낳는 기계가 아닌 것처럼
아내는 나의 몸종이 아니고
평등하게 사랑하는 친구이며 부부라는 것을
우리의 모든 관계는 신뢰와 존중과
민주주의에 바탕해야 한다는 것을
잔업 끝내고 돌아올 아내를 기다리며

이불홑청을 꿰매면서
아픈 각성의 바늘을 찌른다

얼마짜리지

말더듬이 염색공 사촌 형은
10년 퇴직금을 중동취업 브로커에게 털리고 나서
자살을 했다
돈 100만 원이면
아파 누우신 우리 엄마 병원을 가고
스물아홉 노처녀 누나 꽃가말 탄다
돈 천만 원이면
내가 10년을 꼬박 벌어야 한다
1억 원은 두 번 태어나 발버둥 쳐도 엄두도 나지 않는
강 건너 산 너머 무지개이다
나의 인생은 일당 4,000원짜리
그대의 인생은 얼마
우리 사장님은 하룻밤 술값이 100만 원이래는데
강아지 하루 식대가 5,000원이래는데
3천억을 쥐고 흔든 여장부도 있다는데
염색공 사촌 형은 120만 원에 자살을 하고
열여섯 우리 동생 공장을 가고
오 오
우리의 인생 우리의 사랑 우리의 생명은

얼마 얼마?

어디로 갈꺼나

어디로 갈꺼나
눈부시게 푸르른 오월
얼마 만에 찾아 먹는 휴일인데
정순이는 오늘도 특근이란다
어디로 갈꺼나
프로야구 중계도 끝난
테레비도 싱거워
전자오락실에서 동전 몇 닢 쏭쏭 날리고
이 거리 저 거리 돌아다니기도 지쳐
시원한 생맥주 한 잔 하고
영화라도 한 편 보고
디스코장에라도 가고 싶은데
벌써 가불이 오만 원째다
무엇을 할꺼나
얼마 만의 휴일인데
자꾸만 초조해
편지도 못 쓰겠고 책도 안 잡히고
에라 장기판 두드리다
짤짤이나 하다가 그도 시진하여

쥐포에 소주잔을 돌리면서도
무언가 해야 하는데,
어디론가 가야 하는데,

등산친목회도 축구동우회도
한자공부도 독서모임도
잔업에 밀려 휴일특근에 깨져
아무것도 계획할 수 없어,
이러다간 삼 주째 못 본
사랑스런 정순이마저
날아가 버릴지 몰라

사장님은 교양 때마다
놀면 돈만 쓰니 젊을 때 열심히
잔업에다 휴일특근 시키는 대로
다 여러분 위해서 가족처럼 말씀하시고
제미랄 좆도!
안 쓰고 안 먹고
조출철야 휴일특근 몸부림쳐도

가불액만 늘어가고,
계획은 조각나 버려
아 그렇게도 기다리던 휴일날,
어디로 갈꺼나
갈 곳이 없다
무엇을 할꺼나
할 돈이 없구나
대책을 세울 수 없어
이 눈부신 신록의 오월에
우리는 빈속 소주잔에 비틀거리며
슬픔을 마신다
분노를 마신다
쓰디쓴 노동자의 비애를 마신다

한강

한강이 가슴을 연다
여윈 어미의 가슴처럼
주름진 강심(江心)이 소리 없이 열려 흐른다

얼어붙은 겨울 속으로
숨죽이며 흐느낌으로 흐르던
눈물 강물

봄은 멀은데
멍든 가슴, 지치인 노동에
탄식하며 탄식하며 쓰러져
몰아치는 찬바람에
다시 아귀찬 이를 물며 일어서 흐르는
사랑이여 모진 생명이여

강물은 흐르고
더러움과 오욕에 뒤섞여
거칠게 한강은 흐르고

살얼음을 뒤척이며
어두운 겨울 속으로
봄을 부르며
봄을 부르며
소리 없이 열려 흐르는
눈물이여 강물이여

그리움

공장 뜨락에
다사론 봄볕 내리면
휴일이라 생기 도는 아이들 얼굴 위로
개나리 꽃눈이 춤추며 난다

하늘하늘 그리움으로
노오란 작은 손
꽃바람 자락에 날려 보내도
더 그리워 그리워서
온몸 흔들다
한 방울 눈물로 떨어진다

바람 드세도
모락모락 아지랑이로 피어나
온 가슴을 적셔 오는 그리움이여
스물다섯 청춘 위로
미싱 바늘처럼 꼭꼭 찍혀 오는
가난에 울며 떠나던
아프도록 그리운 사람아

포장마차

모래에 싹이 텄나
사장님이 애를 뱄나
이 좋은 토요일 잔업이 없단다

이태리타올로 기름 낀 손을 닦고서
작업복 갈아입고 담배 한 대 붙여 물면
두둥실 풍선처럼 마음이 들떠
누구라 할 것 없이 한 잔 꺾자며
공장 뒷담 포장마차 커튼을 연다
쇠주파 막걸리파 편을 가르다
다수결 두꺼비로 통일을 보고
첫딸 본 김형 추켜 꼼장어 굽고
새신랑 정형 얼러대어
정력에 좋다고 해삼 한 접시
자격증 시험 붙어 호봉 올라간
문형이 기분 조오타고 족발 두 개 사고
걸게 놓인 안주발에 절로 술이 익는다

새벽에 안 서는 놈은 빚도 주지 말랬는데

잔업에 곯다 보니 요게 새벽까지 기척도 안 해
일주일째 아내 고것 곰팡이 슬겠다고 킬킬거리고,
이제 신혼 한 달째인 정형 새 신부
토실한 히프 모양이 첫아들 날 상이라며
좌우삼삼 일심구천 김형 5단계 노하우 전수에
헤 벌리는 놈, 심각한 놈, 키득대는 놈,
한 잔 두 잔 술잔이 돌아올 때마다
우리는 녹아들어 하나가 되어
송형은 문형에게 감정풀이 화해주를 청하고
서씨는 전기과 박형과 찜찜했던 오해를 털어놓고
노씨는 왕년에 광빨나던 시절 타령이 시작되고
장단 맞추는 김형, 만주에서 개장수하며 독립운동하던
뻥까는 야화가 기세를 올리면 부산 자갈치 공형,
야야 치라 치라 벌써 백 번째다 마
내 한 곡 뽑제, 니 박수 안 치나
두만강을 노 저어 오륙도 돌아
개나리 처녀 미워 미워
울고 넘는 박달재로 발길을 돌려
젓가락 두들기며 주전자 뚜껑 드럼에도

어깨 우쭐, 방뎅이 들썩,
쿵다라 닥닥 조코 좋커
영자야 안주 한 사라 더 주라 잉

2차 가자 집에 가자 고고장 가자는 걸
알뜰꾼 신씨가 눌러 앉히고 한 병 두 병 더할수록
거나하게 취기가 올라
좆 같은 노무과장, 상무새끼, 쪽발이 사장놈,
노사협의회 놈들 때려 엎자고
꼭 닫아둔 울화통들이 터져 나온다
문형은 간신자식들 먼저 깨야 한다며
벌겋게 달아오르고
정형은 단계적으로 구내식당부터
시정하자고 나직이 속삭인다

상고 나와 기름쟁이 된 회계담당 김형은
외상장부 넘겨 가며
계산을 한다
냉수 한 사발 돌려 마시고

자욱한 연기 속 포장마차 나서면
어깨를 끼고 비틀비틀
일렬횡대로 서 담벽에 오줌 깔기고
씨팔, 내일도 휴일특근 나온다며
리어카 장수 떨이쳐 딸기 천 원어치씩
옆주머니에 꿰차고
작별의 손 흔들며 잔업 없는 오늘만은
두둥실 토요일 밤을 흥얼거리며
아내가 기다리는 집을 향한다

가리봉 시장

가리봉 시장에 밤이 깊으면
가게마다 내걸어 놓은 백열전등 불빛 아래
오가는 사람들의 상기된 얼굴마다
따스한 열기가 오른다

긴 노동 속에 갇혀 있던
우리는 자유로운 새가 되어
이리 기웃 저리 기웃 깔깔거리고
껀수 찾는 어깨들도 뿌리뽑힌 전과자도
몸 부벼 살아가는 술집여자들도
눈을 빛내며 열이 오른다

돈이 생기면 제일 먼저 가리봉 시장을 찾아
친한 친구랑 떡볶이 500원어치, 김밥 한 접시,
기분 나면 살짝이 생맥주 한 잔이면
스테이크 잡수시는 사장님 배만큼 든든하고
천오백 원짜리 티샤쓰 색깔만 고우면
친구들은 환한 내 얼굴이 귀티 난다고 한다

하루 14시간
손발이 퉁퉁 붓도록
유명브랜드 비싼 옷을 만들어도
고급오디오 조립을 해도
우리 몫은 없어,
우리 손으로 만들고도 엄두도 못 내
가리봉 시장으로 몰려와
하청공장에서 막 뽑아낸 싸구려 상품을
눈부시게 구경하며
이번 달엔 큰맘 먹고 물색 원피스나
한 벌 사야겠다고 다짐을 한다

앞판 시다 명지는 이번 월급 타면
켄터키치킨 한 접시 먹으면 소원이 없겠다 하고
마무리 때리는 정이는 2,800원짜리
이쁜 샌달 하나 보아둔 게 있다며
잔업 없는 날 시장 가자고 손을 꼽는다

가리봉 시장에 밤이 익으면,

피가 마르게 온 정성으로
만든 제품을
화려한 백화점으로,
물 건너 코 큰 나라로 보내고 난
허기지고 지친
우리 공돌이 공순이들이
싸구려 상품을 샘나게 찍어 두며
300원어치 순대 한 접시로 허기를 달래고
이리 기웃 저리 기웃
구경만 하다가
허탈하게 귀갓길로
발길을 돌린다

지문을 부른다

진눈깨비 속을
웅크려 헤쳐 나가며 작업시간에
가끔 이렇게 일 보러 나오면
참말 좋겠다고 웃음 나누며
우리는 동회로 들어선다

초라한 스물아홉 사내의
사진 껍질을 벗기며
가리봉동 공단에 묻힌 지가
어언 육 년, 세월은 밤낮으로 흘러
뜻도 없이 죽음처럼 노동 속에 흘러
한 번쯤은 똑같은 국민임을 확인하며
주민등록 경신을 한다

평생토록 죄진 적 없이
이 손으로 우리 식구 먹여 살리고
수출품을 생산해 온
검고 투박한 자랑스런 손을 들어
지문을 찍는다

아
없어, 선명하게
없어,
노동 속에 문드러져
너와 나 사람마다 다르다는
지문이 나오지를 않아
없어, 정형도 이형도 문형도
사라져 버렸어
임석경찰은 화를 내도
긴 노동 속에
물 건너간 수출품 속에 묻혀
지문도, 청춘도, 존재마저
사라져 버렸나 봐

몇 번이고 찍어 보다
끝내 지문이 나오지 않는 화공약품 공장
아가씨들은 끝내 울음이 북받치고
줄지어 나오는, 지문 나오지 않는 사람들끼리
우리는 존재조차 없어

강도질해도 흔적도 남지 않을 거라며
정형이 농지껄여도
더 이상 아무도 웃지 않는다

지문 없는 우리들은
얼어붙은 침묵으로
똑같은 국민임을 되뇌이며
파편으로 내리꽂히는 진눈깨비 속을 헤쳐
공단 속으로 묻혀져 간다
선명하게 되살아날
지문을 부르며
노동자의 푸르른 생명을 부르며
되살아날
너와 나의 존재
노동자의 새봄을
부르며 부르며
진눈깨비 속으로,
타오르는 갈망으로 간다

영어회화

우리 오매 일찍이 홀몸으로
논 서 마지기 농약 뿌리다
허연 두 눈 치뜨고 돌아가시고
두견이 피 토하는 울음을 뒤로
서울로 캄캄하게 떠나올 제에
누나 따라간다며 숙모 손을 뿌리치고
치맛자락 매달리던 코흘리개 영석이가
어느새 중학생이 되어
영어회화 듣기평가 시험에
카세트 테이프가 없어서
잘사는 집 애들보다 점수가 뒤진다며
자정이 넘도록 영어책을 읽다가
잠꼬대로까지 중얼거린다

누나는 미국 전자회사
공순이가 되었어도
세컨라인 리더가 되어
QC활동에 목이 붓도록
칼처럼 곤두세워 오버타임을 더 해도

다음 달엔 우리 영석이
카세트랑 테이프는 꼭 사서 주마
잔업 끝난 자정거리 휘청거려 오면
하지 말라 화를 내고 다짐을 해도
영석이는 서툰 솜씨로 밥을 지어 차려 놓고
낭랑하게 꼬부라진
영어회화 공부를 한다

누나는 못 배워서
무식한 공순이지만
영석이 너만은 공부 잘해서
꼭 꼭 훌륭한 사람 되거라
하지만 영석아
남 위에 올라서서
피눈물 흘리게 하지는 말아라

네가 영어공부에 열중할 때마다
누나는 노조에서 배운
우리나라 역사가 생각난다

부유층 아들딸들이 유치원서부터
영어회화 교육에다
외국인 학교 나가고
중학생인 네가 잠꼬대로까지
영어회화 중얼거리고
거리 간판이나 상표까지
꼬부랑 글씨 천지인데
테레비나 라디오에서도
영어회화쯤 매끈하게 굴릴 수 있어야
세련되고 교양 있는 현대인이라는데
무식한 공순이 누나는
미국 전자회사 세컨라인 리더 누나는
자꾸만 자꾸만 노조에서 배운
우리나라 역사가 생각난다

말도, 글도, 성도, 혼도 빼앗아 가고
논도, 밭도, 식량도, 생산물까지
마침내 노동자의 생명까지도
차근차근 침략하던 일제하

조선어 말살
　　　생각이 난다
미국 전자회사 세컨라인 리더 누나는
컨베이어 벨트에 밀려드는 부품에
QC활동에 칼처럼 곤두설수록
조선어 말살
생각이 난다

썩으러 가는 길
―군대 가는 후배에게―

열여섯 앳된 얼굴로
공장문을 들어선 지 5년 세월을
밤낮으로 기계에 매달려
잘 먹지도 잘 놀지도 남은 것 하나 없이
설운 기름밥에 몸부림하던 그대가
싸나이로 태어나서 이제 군대를 가는구나
한참 좋은 청춘을 썩으러 가는구나

굵은 눈물 흘리며
떠나가는 그대에게
이 못난 선배는 줄 것이 없다
쓴 소주 이별 잔밖에는 줄 것이 없다
하지만 철수야
그대는 썩으러 가는 것이 아니다
푸른 제복에 갇힌 3년 세월 어느 하루도
헛되이 버릴 수 없는 고귀한 삶이다

그대는 군에서도 열심히 살아라

행정반이나 편안한 보직을 탐내지 말고
동료들 속에서도 열외 치지 말아라
똑같이 군복 입고 똑같이 짬밥 먹고
똑같이 땀 흘리는 군대생활 속에서도
많이 배우고 가진 놈들의 치사한 처세 앞에
오직 성실성과 부지런한 노동으로만
당당하게 인정을 받아라

빗자루 한 번 더 들고
식기 한 개 더 닦고
작업할 땐 열심으로
까라면 까고 뽑으라면 뽑고
요령 피우지 말고 적극적으로 살아라
고참들의 횡포나 윗동기의 한따까리가
억울할지 몰라도
혼자서만 헛고생한다고 회의할지 몰라도
세월 가면 그대도 고참이 되는 것,
차라리 저임금에 노동을 팔며
갈수록 늘어나는 잔업에 바둥치는 이놈의 사회보단

평등하게 돌고 도는 군대생활이
오히려 공평하고 깨끗하지 않으냐
그 속에서 비굴을 넘어선 인종을 배우고
공동을 위해 다 함께 땀 흘리는 참된 노동을 배워라

몸으로 움직이는 실천적 사랑과
궂은일 마다않는 희생정신으로
그대는 좋은 벗들을 찾고 만들어라
돈과 학벌과 빽줄로 판가름나는 사회 속에서
똑같이 쓰라린 상처 입은 벗들끼리
오직 성실과 부지런한 노동만이
진실하고 소중한 가치임을 온몸으로 일깨워
끈끈한 협동 속에 하나가 되는 또 다른 그대,
좋은 벗들을 얻어라

걸진 웃음 속에 모험과 호기를 펼치고
유격과 행군과 한따까리 속에 깡다구를 기르고
명령의 진위를 분별하여 행하는 용기와
쫄따구를 감싸 주는 포용력을 넓혀라

시간 나면 읽고 생각하고 반성하며
열심히 학습하거라
달빛 쏟아지는 적막한 초소 아래서
분단의 비극을 깊이깊이 새기거라

그대는 울면서
군대 3년을 썩으러 가는구나
썩어 다시 꽃망울로
돌아올 날까지
열심히 썩어라

이 못난 선배도 그대도 벗들도
눈부신 꽃망울로 피어나
온 세상을 환히 뒤흔들 때까지
우리 모두 함께
열심히 썩자
그리하여 달궈지고 다듬어진
튼실한 일꾼으로
노동과 실천과 협동성이

생활 속에 배인 좋은 벗들과 함께
빛나는 얼굴로
우리 품에 돌아오라

철수야 눈물을 닦아라
노동자의 끈질긴 생명력으로
열심히 열심히
잘 썩어야 한다

남성편력기

시다 시절
훤칠한 미남에다
눈매와 뒷모습이 사슴처럼 쓸쓸해 뵈는
검사반 진수가 좋아
밤늦도록 그 가을을 함께 걸었지만
갈수록 내 가슴은 마른 낙엽이었지

미싱사가 되어
미치게 배우고 싶어
셋집 주인네 친절한 대학생을 사모하여
지친 몸으로 새벽까지 책을 읽어도
그와 나 사이엔 메울 수 없는
깊은 강이 흐르고 있었다

조장이 되어
돈 잘 쓰고 세련미가 멋져
지시할 때 위엄 있고 인간미 넘치는 김과장이 좋아
경양식집 조명불빛 아래 웃음 지어 봤지만
허망한 한 잔 맥주 거품이었지

내 불안한 존재를 듬직하게 안아 줄
남자답고 야성적인 정열이와의 겨울은
상처 입은 고목처럼 거친 아픔이었다

반장이 되었을 때
동갑내기들이 결혼에 들뜨고
성실하고 가정적인 영훈씨와의 사랑도
제 한 몸밖에 모르는 이기와 독선에 질려
갈 테면 가라고 떠나 보냈지

미싱밥 8년에
백여 명이던 회사가 천오백 명으로
대회사로 늘어났으나
내게 남은 것은 50만 원짜리 월세 한 칸
월부 카세트 하나
그리고 진이 빠진 스물다섯 육신

토닥거리는 주임의 격려와 부장님의 회식이 있고 나면
어김없이 조여드는 생산량에

미싱사 시다를 달달 볶으며
정신없이 밟아 대고 악을 쓰다가
잔업 끝난 밤거리를 천근 무게로 지쳐 가면서
이래서는 안 된다
이것이 아니다
이를 깨물며 다짐해 본다

점심 후 재단반에 바람이 일어
2년째 얼어붙은 임금 50% 인상하라
주저앉아 제끼고
국만이는 나를 붙들고
단결하면 이길 수 있다고, 더 이상 이용당하지 말자고
눈을 빛내면서 설득을 한다

나의 두 눈에 눈물이 맺히고
우리는 현장을 돌며
메마른 가슴들을 한 덩어리로
뜨겁게 일으켜 세워
전쟁터 같은 현장은 일시에 긴장된 침묵만이 감돌고

허둥대며 퍼렇게 고함치는 주임 부장의 발악에도
내 가슴은 난생처음 평온한 대지가 되어
생명의 죽순이 파랗게 기운차 오른다

연약하고 우스갯소리만 잘하는 줄 알았던 국만이가
저렇듯 동료들의 깊은 신뢰 속에
확실한 주관과 실천력이 있음이
가진 사장보다 더 당당한 용기와 뚜렷한 소신으로
희생을 각오한 큰 사랑을 키워 가고 있음이
3일간의 싸움 속에서
뜨거운 감명으로 충만되어 젖어 온다

참다운 남자란 이런 남자라고
일생을 함께하며 내 모든 것을 다 주어도
기쁨으로 살아날 진짜 남자라고
어떤 고난도 함께 싸워나가리라고
두근거리는 가슴을 안으며
활시위처럼 팽팽하게
나를 가다듬는다

모를 이야기들

갈수록 수출이 어려워지고
나라 빚이 세계에서 세 번째라는데
소비를 억제하고 저축을 하자는데
물가를 꼭 붙들어야 한다는데
잔업에 지쳐 온 나에게
테레비에선 예쁜 여자가
VTR, 오디오, 에어컨을 광고하며
최소한 칼라TV에 냉장고 세탁기는
필수품이라고, 요염한 미소를 던지며
차원 있게 먹고 입고 쓰라고 한다

10분간의 휴식시간에
우리는 옹기종기 담배를 나누며
요즘 세상사가 뭐가 뭔지 모르겠다며
하여튼 노동자만 점점 죽어난다고 탄식한다
정말 뭐가 뭔지 모르겠다
나라 형편이 이리도 어려운데

농토 메꾼 골프장엔 대낮에도 자가용이 가득 차고

콘도미니엄이 불타나고 유명브랜드 로열티가 늘어나고
고급 중형 승용차는 생산이 딸리고
사우나 안마소가, 호텔이 곳곳에 솟아나고
고급 요정 요릿집이 불야성을 이루고
수십억 들여 세계 미인대회, 가요제, 운동경기 유치하고
정말 이래도 되는 건지 겁만 난다

신문에선 물가가 제자리 숫자라는데
주인네는 셋돈을 올려 달라 하고
공공요금 고지서가 무거워만 가고
아내는 시장에 다녀올 때마다
가벼워진 바구니를 들며 울상이다
임금동결 정책에 넋을 잃다가
매주 4시간을 더 연장노동해도
적자가계부를 들여다보며
아내는 어두운 한숨이 늘고
프로야구장엔 환호가 일고
프로축구장엔 열기가 뜨겁고
우린 정말 뭐가 뭔지 모르겠다

높은 외국 나리들이 줄지어 방한하여
번영과 발전상에 감탄을 하고
국민소득이 늘고 대기업이 더 커지고
호화로운 빌딩이 줄지어 서고
88올림픽이 온 세계를 부르고
정의로운 복지사회가 정착되었다는데
우리는 임금동결에 묶여
날이 갈수록 노동시간만 늘어나고
후들거리는 몸을 가눠
캄캄한 번영의 뒤안길을
떨며 무겁게 지쳐서 간다
—대학생들은 민주주의를 부르짖고,
 옆 회사 동료는 숨죽여 속삭이며
 민주노조 소문을 전하고—

통박

어느 놈이 커피 한 잔 산다 할 때는
뭔가 바라는 게 있다는 걸 안다

고상하신 양반이
부드러운 미소로 내 등을 두드릴 땐
내게 무얼 원하는지 안다

별스런 대우와 칭찬에
허릴 굽신이며 감격해도
저들이 내게 무얼 노리는지 안다

우리들이 일어설 때
노사협조를 되뇌이며 물러서는
저 인자한 웃음 뒤의 음모와 칼날을
우리는 안다

유식하고 높은 양반들만이 지혜로운 것은 아니다
일찍이 세상바다 뒹굴며
눈칫밥을 익히며 헤아릴 수 없는 배신과 패배 속에

세상 살아가는 통박이 생기드만

세상엔 빡빡 기는 놈들 위에서
신선처럼 너울너울 나는 놈 따로 있어
날개 없이 기름바다 기는 우리야
움츠리며 통박을 굴리며 살아가지만
통박이 구르다 보면
통박끼리 구르고 합쳐지다 보면
거대한 통박이 된다고

좆도 배운 것 없어도
돈날개 칼날개 달고 설치는 놈들이 무엇인지
이놈의 세상이 어찌 된 세상인지
누구를 위한 세상인지
우리들 거대한 통박으로 안다

쓰라린 눈물과 억압과 패배 속에서
거대한 통박으로 구르고 부딪치고 합치면서
우리들의 통박은

점점 날카롭고 명확하게
가다듬어지는 것이다

우리들의 통박이 거대한 통박으로,
하나의 통박으로 뭉쳐지면서
노동하는 우리들의 새날을 향하여
이놈의 세상을 굴려갈 것이다

바겐세일

오늘도 공단거리 찾아 헤맨다마는
검붉은 노을이 서울 하늘 뒤덮을 때까지
찾아 헤맨다마는
없구나 없구나
스물일곱 이 한목숨
밥 벌 자리 하나 없구나

토큰 한 개 달랑, 포장마차 막소주잔에 가슴 적시고
뿌리 없는 웃음 흐르는 아스팔트 위를
반짝이는 조명불빛 사이로
허청허청
실업자로 걷는구나

10년 걸려 목메인 기름밥에
나의 노동은 일당 4,000원
오색영롱한 쇼윈도엔 온통 바겐세일 나붙고
지하도 옷장수 500원짜리 쉰 목청이 잦아들고
내 손목 이끄는 밤꽃의 하이얀 미소도
50% 바겐세일이구나

에라 씨팔,
나도 바겐세일이다
3,500원도 좋고 3,000원도 좋으니 팔려가라
바겐세일로 바겐세일로
다만,
내 이 슬픔도 절망도 분노까지 함께 사야 돼!

시다의 꿈

긴 공장의 밤
시린 어깨 위로
피로가 한파처럼 몰려온다

드르륵 득득
미싱을 타고, 꿈결 같은 미싱을 타고
두 알의 타이밍으로 철야를 버티는
시다의 언 손으로
장밋빛 꿈을 잘라
이룰 수 없는 헛된 꿈을 싹뚝 잘라
피 흐르는 가죽본을 미싱대에 올린다
끝도 없이 올린다

아직은 시다
미싱대에 오르고 싶다
미싱을 타고
장군처럼 당당한 얼굴로 미싱을 타고
언 몸뚱아리 감싸 줄
따스한 옷을 만들고 싶다

찢겨진 살림을 깁고 싶다

떨려 오는 온몸을 소름 치며
가위질 망치질로 다림질하는
아직은 시다,
미싱을 타고 미싱을 타고
갈라진 세상 모오든 것들을
하나로 연결하고 싶은
시다의 꿈으로
찬바람 치는 공단거리를
허청이며 내달리는
왜소한 시다의 몸짓
파리한 이마 위로
새벽별 빛나다

봄

허기진 배를 쓸며
오전 내 기다린 점심시간이면
공장뜰 귀퉁이에도 봄볕이 따사롭다

아직 시려운 시멘트벽에 어깨를 기대고
배불러 이야기 많은 아이들 속에서
사르르 졸리운 눈을 들면
가물가물 피어오르는 아지랑이처럼
고향집 그리운 추억이 흔들린다

못 먹고 부친 돈으로 빚은 얼마나 갚았을까
주름진 어머님의 손등, 고랑 깊은 아버지의 검게 탄 얼굴
철없이 보채고 웃고 싸울 동생들의 모습이
진달래 꽃잎처럼 선연하다

독한 추위도 독한 고생도 그보다 더 독하게 이 악물며
겨우내 많이도 기다린 이 봄,
거리에 나서면
봄빛 고운 새 옷도 입고 싶고

싫도록 배불리 맛난 것 먹고 싶지만
착하게 성실하게 모든 것을 견뎌 보겠노라
꼬옥 입술 깨물 때
때르르르릉——
오후 작업벨 소리에 빨려가는
숙이의 종종걸음을
봄바람이 살랑 띄우고 간다

졸음

선적날짜가 다가오면
백리길 천리길도 쉬임없이 몰아치는
강행군이 시작된다
어차피 하지 말라 해도
올라간 방세를 메꾸려면
아파서 밀린 곗돈을 때우려면
주 78시간이건, 84시간은 먹어치워야 한다

전생에 일 못하고 잠 못 잔 귀신이 씌웠나
꼬집어도 찔러도 혀를 깨물어도
고된 피로의 바다 졸음의 물결에
꼴까닥 꼴까닥
눈앞에는 프레스의 허연 칼날이 쓰을컹 툭탁
미싱 때려 밟는 순정이는
눈감고도 죽죽 누비는 자동기계가 되어
망치질하는 어린 시다
깨어진 손을 감싸 울면서도
눈이 감긴다

작업장 스피커에선
마이클 잭슨의 괴성,
조용필의 흐느낌이 지침 없이 흘러나오고
주임 과장이 악을 써대도
졸음은 밑도 끝도 없이 휘감아들어
차라리 차라리 우린
자동기계가 되었으면,
잠 안 자는 짐승이 되기를 원하며
피 흐르는 손가락을 묶는다

아침에도 대낮에도 밤중에도
단 한 순간 맑은 날이 없이
미치게 미치게 졸려,
꿈결 속에 노동하며 아직 성하게
용케도 붙어 있는 내 두 손이 고맙구나
시커먼 무우짠지처럼
피로와 졸음에 절여진 스물일곱 청춘,
그래도 아침이면 코피 쏟으며 일어나
졸음보다 더 굵다란

저임금의 포승줄에 끌려
햇살도 찬란한 번영의 새 아침을
졸며 절며
지옥 같은 전쟁터
저주스러운 기계 앞에
꿇어앉는다

휴일특근

4시간 연장노동 끝에
서둘러 밤차를 타고
어둔 골목길을 더듬어 방문을 들어서면
귀염둥이 민주는 벌써 꿈나라 아기별이 되었다

일주일째 아빠 얼굴을 못 보더니,
오늘 저녁엔 꼬옥 아빠를 보고 잔다고
색칠놀이 그림 그리기로 잠을 쫓기에
내일은 일요일이라 아빠랑 놀러 가자고 달래 재웠다며
아내는 엷게 웃는다

올해도 임금은 오르지 않고
주인네는 전셋돈을 50만 원은 더 올려 달라 하고
이번 달엔 어머님 제사가 있고
다음 달엔 명선이 결혼식이고
내년엔 우리 민주 유치원도 보내야 한다

이대로 세 몸뚱아리 아프지만 않는다면
김치에 밥만 먹고 아무 일만 없다면

매주 78시간 꾸준히 버텨 나간다면
열 달 남은 100만 원짜리 계는 끝낼 수 있으련만
올봄 들어 유난히 심해진 현기증에
외줄을 타는 듯 불안하다

벽에 걸린 달력을 보며
빨간 숫자는 아빠 쉬는 날이라고
민주는 크레용으로 이번 달에 6개나
동그라미를 그려 놓았다

민주야
저 달력의 빨간 숫자는
아빠의 휴일이 아니란다
배부르고 능력 있는 양반들의 휴일이지
곤히 잠든 민주야
너만은 훌륭하게 키우려고
네가 손꼽아 기다리며 동그라미 쳐논
빨간 휴일날 아빠는 특근을 간다
발걸음도 무거운 창백한 얼굴로

화창한 신록의 휴일을 비켜
특근을 간다

선진조국 노동자
민주 아빠는
저임금의 올가미에 모가지가 매여서
빨간 휴일날
누렇게 누렇게 찌들은 소처럼
휴일특근을 간다 민주야

손 무덤

올 어린이날만은
안사람과 아들놈 손목 잡고
어린이 대공원에라도 가야겠다며
은하수를 빨며 웃던 정형의
손목이 날아갔다

작업복을 입었다고
사장님 그라나다 승용차도
공장장님 로얄살롱도
부장님 스텔라도 태워 주지 않아
한참 피를 흘린 후에
타이탄 짐칸에 앉아 병원을 갔다

기계 사이에 끼어 아직 팔딱거리는 손을
기름 먹은 장갑 속에서 꺼내어
36년 한 많은 노동자의 손을 보며 말을 잊는다

비닐봉지에 싼 손을 품에 넣고
봉천동 산동네 정형 집을 찾아

서글한 눈매의 그의 아내와 초롱한 아들놈을 보며
차마 손만은 꺼내 주질 못하였다

훤한 대낮에 산동네 구멍가게 주저앉아 쇠주병을 비우고
정형이 부탁한 산재 관계 책을 찾아
종로의 크다는 책방을 둘러봐도
엠병할, 산데미 같은 책들 중에
노동자가 읽을 책은 두 눈 까뒤집어도 없고

화창한 봄날 오후의 종로거리엔
세련된 남녀들이 화사한 봄빛으로 흘러가고
영화에서 본 미국 상가처럼
외국상표 찍힌 왼갖 좋은 것들이 휘황하여
작업화를 신은 내가
마치 탈출한 죄수처럼 쫄드만

고층 사우나 빌딩 앞엔 자가용이 즐비하고
고급 요정 살롱 앞에도 승용차가 가득하고
거대한 백화점이 넘쳐흐르고

프로야구장엔 함성이 일고
노동자들이 칼처럼 곤두세워 좆 빠져라 일할 시간에
느긋하게 즐기는 년놈들이 왜 이리 많은지
— 원하는 것은 무엇이든 얻을 수 있고
　　바라는 것은 무엇이든 이룰 수 있는 —
선진조국의 종로거리를
나는 ET가 되어
얼나간 미친놈처럼 헤매이다
일당 4,800원짜리 노동자로 돌아와
연장노동 도장을 찍는다

내 품속의 정형 손은
싸늘히 식어 푸르뎅뎅하고
우리는 손을 소주에 씻어 들고
양지바른 공장 담벼락 밑에 묻는다
노동자의 피땀 위에서
번영의 조국을 향락하는 누런 착취의 손들을
일 안 하고 놀고먹는 하얀 손들을
묻는다

프레스로 싹둑싹둑 짓짤라
원한의 눈물로 묻는다
일하는 손들이
기쁨의 손짓으로 살아날 때까지
묻고 또 묻는다

어쩌면

어쩌면 나는 기계인지도 몰라
컨베이어에 밀려오는 부품을
정신없이 납땜하다 보면
수천 번이고 로버트처럼 반복동작하는
나는 기계가 되어 버렸는지도 몰라

어쩌면 우리는 양계장 닭인지도 몰라
라인마다 쪼로록 일렬로 앉아
희끄무레한 불빛 아래 속도에 따라 손을 놀리고
빠른 음악을 틀어 주면 알을 더 많이 낳는
양계장 닭인지도 몰라
진이 빠져 더 이상 알을 못 낳으면
폐닭이 되어 켄터키치킨이 되는
양계장 닭인지도 몰라

늘씬한 정순이는 이렇게 살아 무엇하냐며
맥주홀로 울며 떠나고
영남이는 위장병에 괴로워하다
한 마리 폐닭이 되어 황폐한 고향으로 떠난다

3년 내내 아귀차게 이 악물며 야간학교 마친 재심이는
경리 자리라도 알아보다가 졸업장을 찢으며 주저앉는다
어쩌면 우리는 멍에 쓴 짐승인지도 몰라

저들은,
알 빼먹는 저들은
어쩌면 날강도인지도 몰라
인간을 기계로
　　　소모품으로
　　　　상품으로 만들어 버리는
점잖고 합법적인 날강도인지도 몰라

저 자상한 미소도
세련된 아름다움과 교양도
부유하고 찬란한 광휘도
어쩌면 우리 것인지도 몰라
우리들의 피눈물과 절망과 고통 위에서
우리들의 웃음과 아름다움과 빛을
송두리째 빨아먹는

어쩌면 저들은 흡혈귀인지도 몰라

당신을 버릴 때

첫사랑의 소박한 그녀를
내가 겉멋 들어 버렸을 때
희뿌연 가로등 아래서
그녀는 잡지도 않고 말 한마디 없이
굵은 눈물 흘리며 천천히 기숙사로 돌아갔다

내가 세상을 알았을 때
소박하고 진실한 그녀는
저만큼 앞서 해고자가 되어
또다시 어느 현장에 몸을 담고
어리석은 나를
조용히 미소 지으며 손짓하고 있었다

2년을 바둥쳐 봐도 얼어붙은 이 침묵
잠들은 동료들을 병신이라 원망하고
자포자기한 동료들을 흔들어 봐도
움직이지 않는 죽음의 바다 앞에서
몸도 마음도 지쳐 버렸다

십 년을 노력해도 가망 없다고
차라리 다른 곳에 씨를 뿌리자고
사직서를 품에 넣고 출근한 아침
웅성웅성 동료들은 일손을 놓고
눈과 눈을 마주쳐 불꽃이 일고
말과 가슴이 합쳐져 함성으로
처얼썩 출렁 파도쳐
천이백 근육들의 출렁임으로
거대한 해일처럼 휩쓸며
일어서던 날,

내가 눈이 어두워
그녀를 버린 것처럼
나는 형제를 믿지 못하였었다

우리는 기계가 아닌 인간임을
억눌리고 빼앗기는 노동자임을
견디다 못해 일어서면 해일이 되는
무겁고 깊은 바다임을

나는 매몰 속에서
섣부른 머리와 조급함으로
지루함을 이기지 못하고
형제를 버리려 했었다

숨죽인 바다는
마침내 해일이 되는 것을,
굳센 믿음으로 옳은 실천으로
끈질긴 집념으로
서둘지 말자
그러나 쉬지도 말자

진짜 노동자

한세상 살면서
뼈 빠지게 노동하면서
아득바득 조출철야 매달려도
돌아오는 건 쥐씨알만한지

죽어라 생산하는 놈
인간답게 좀 살라꼬 몸부림쳐도
죽어랏 쇳가루만 날아들고 콱콱 막히고
꼴프채 비껴찬 신선놀음허는 놈들
불도쟈처럼 정력 좋은 이윤추구에는 비까번쩍 애국갈채
제미랄 세상사가 왜 이리 불평등한지

이 땅에 노동자로 태어나서
생각도 못 하고 사는 놈은 죽은 송장이여
말도 못 하는 놈은 썩은 괴기여
테레비만 좋아라 믿는 놈은 얼빠진 놈
이빨만 까는 놈은 좆도 헛물
실천하는 사람,
동료들 속에서 살아 움직이며 실천하는 노동자만이

진실로 인간이제
진짜 노동자이제

비암이라고 다 비암이 아니여
독이 있어야 비암이지
쎈방이라고 다 쎈방이 아녀
바이트가 달려야 쎈방이지
노동자라고 다 노동자가 아니제
동료와 어깨를 꼭 끼고 성큼성큼 나아가
불도쟈 밀어제껴 우리 것 찾아 담는
포크레인 삽날 정도는 되아야
진짜 노동자지

평온한 저녁을 위하여

나면서부터인가
노동자가 된 후부터인가
내 영혼은 불안하다

새벽잠을 깨면
또다시 시작될 하루의 노동
거대한 기계의 매정한 회전
주임놈의 차가운 낯짝이
어둠처럼 덮쳐 오고
아마도 내가 자살한다면
새벽일 거야

잔업 끝난 늦은 귀갓길
산다는 것, 노동자로 산다는 것의
깊은 불안이 또다시 나를 감싼다

화창한 일요일
가족들과 오붓한 저녁상의 웃음 속에서도
보장 없는 내일에

짙은 불안이 엄습해 온다

이 세상에 태어나
죄진 적도 없고
노예살이 머슴살이하는 것도 아닌데
풍요로운 웃음이 하늘에 닿는
안정과 번영의 대한민국 땅에서
떳떳하게 생산하며 살아가는데
왜 이리 종놈처럼 불안한 세상살이인가

믿을 거라곤 이 근육덩어리 하나
착한 아내와 귀여운 딸내미
기만 원짜리 전세 한 칸뿐인데
괴롭기만 한 긴 노동
쪼개고 안 먹고 안 입어도
남는 것 하나 없이 물거품처럼
이러다간 언제 쓰러질지 몰라

상쾌한 아침을 맞아

즐겁게 땀 흘려 노동하고
뉘엿한 석양녘
동료들과 웃음 터뜨리며 공장문을 나서
조촐한 밥상을 마주하는
평온한 저녁을 가질 수는 없는가

떳떳하게 노동하며
평온한 저녁을 갖고 싶은 우리의 꿈을
그 누가 짓밟는가
그 무엇이 우리를 불안케 하는가
불안 속에 살아온 지난 30년을
이제는,
평온한 저녁을 위하여
평온한 미래를 위하여
결코 평온할 수 없는
노동자의 대도(大道)를 따라
불안의 한가운데로 휘저으며
당당하게 당당하게
나아가리라

노동의 새벽

전쟁 같은 밤일을 마치고 난
새벽 쓰린 가슴 위로
차거운 소주를 붓는다
아
이러다간 오래 못 가지
이러다간 끝내 못 가지

설은 세 그릇 짬밥으로
기름투성이 체력전을
전력을 다 짜내어 바둥치는
이 전쟁 같은 노동일을
오래 못 가도
끝내 못 가도
어쩔 수 없지

탈출할 수만 있다면,
진이 빠져, 허깨비 같은
스물아홉의 내 운명을 날아 빠질 수만 있다면
아 그러나

어쩔 수 없지 어쩔 수 없지
죽음이 아니라면 어쩔 수 없지
이 질긴 목숨을,
가난의 멍에를,
이 운명을 어쩔 수 없지

늘어 처진 육신에
또다시 다가올 내일의 노동을 위하여
새벽 쓰린 가슴 위로
차거운 소주를 붓는다
소주보다 독한 깡다구를 오기를
분노와 슬픔을 붓는다

어쩔 수 없는 이 절망의 벽을
기어코 깨뜨려 솟구칠
거치른 땀방울, 피눈물 속에
새근새근 숨 쉬며 자라는
우리들의 사랑
우리들의 분노

우리들의 희망과 단결을 위해
새벽 쓰린 가슴 위로
차거운 소주잔을
돌리며 돌리며 붓는다
노동자의 햇새벽이
솟아오를 때까지

어쩔 수 없지

기름기 없는 설은 세 끼가
뼈다귀까지 녹신한 이 노동일이
내 육신을 골병들게 한다는 걸
나이 들수록 휘청이면서도
어쩔 수 없다

올겨울 들어 세 번째 연탄까스 중독으로
찬 새벽 마당에 엎으러져도
이 셋방살이를 어쩔 수 없다

작업장 소음진동에 가는 귀가 먹고
자욱한 먼지에 폐가 콜콜거려도
어쩔 수 없다

열한 명째 사고가 나고
라면 안주에 소주잔 들고 조용필을 잘 뽑아대던
김씨가 죽던 날도
이젠 떠야겠다고
암만 다짐해 봐도

이 업을 어쩔 수 없다 어쩔 수 없다

그래, 어쩔 수 없다
골병이 들어도 손이 잘려도 죽기까지라도
이 가난을, 노동일을
모진 목숨을 위해선 어쩔 수 없다

산다는 것은
죽어라 일하고 토끼잠에 쫓기고 기름빨래 하고
셋방살이로 떨며
불안과 탄식 속에 사그러드는 것
그래도 우리는 어쩔 수 없다

하늘 같은 사람들은 더 높이 신선이 되고
우리는 점점 작아져도
어쩔 수가, 어쩔 수가 없다

그러나 우리도 사람으로 살기 위해선
어찌할 수 없기에

출렁 처얼썩 파도가 합쳐져
일순간 천지를 뒤엎는
폭풍으로 휘달려올
우리 것 찾는
저 거대한 걸음을, 함성을
어쩔 수 없지
어쩔 수 없지

석양

저 산 넘어 지는 해가
뿌연 유리창으로 붉은 손을 내밀어
눈부시어라 미싱 바늘
자욱이 어른거려 눈 비비며
생산목표 헤아리며
등줄기에 땀이 괴도록 밟는다

오늘은 밀린 빨래, 쌓인 피로
한자공부도 다 제쳐 놓고
연락만 기다린다는 고향친구를 만나
부모님 소식 고향 소식 들으며
회포를 풀어 보자고 열나게
열나게 밟았는데
ㅡ수작 부리지 말고 쓰러지지 않을 지경이면
  잔업 하라고 해ㅡ
주임님의 고함 소리에 노을이
검붉게 탄다

조장언니 성화에

잔업명단 위에 이름이 박히고
아침부터 아프다던 시다 명지는
일감 따라 허덕이며 눈물이 어려
미싱 소리 망치 소리 가르며
라디오 스피커에선
—보람된 하루일과를 마치고 그윽한 한 잔의 커피
와 연인과의 대화 속에 포근한 휴식의 시간, 노을
도 아름답고 산들바람도 싱그러운 저녁입니다. 오
늘도 연예가 산책에 이어 프로야구 소식과 멋진
팝뮤직에 젖어 보세요. 먼저 정수라가 부릅니다.
  아아 우리 대한민국—
이를 갈며,
졸립더라도 꼭 한 장씩 쓰고 자자던
한자공부도 며칠째 흐지부지
생일선물로 받은 소설책도 한 달을 넘긴 채
고향에 편지 쓴 지도 오래
무너지고 세우고 무너진 계획이
헤아릴 수 없어
꺼지는 한숨 속에

산다는 게 뭔지, 울분으로
드륵 드르륵 득득
밟아 댄다

석양은
마지막 검붉은 빛을 토하며
순이의 슬픔도 명지의 눈물도
정자의 울분도 어둠 속으로
무겁게 거두어 간다
그래, 어둠에서 어둠으로
끝없는 노동 속에 절망하고
쓰러지더라도 다시 일어서
슬픈 눈물로 기름 부어 타오르며
우리들 손에 손 맞잡고
사랑과 희망을 버리지 말자
우리 품에 안아야 할
포근한 석양빛의 휴식과 평화
우리들의 권리를 찾을 때까지
슬픔과 절망의 어둠 속에서

마주 잡은 손들을
놓치지 말자

사랑

사랑은
슬픔, 가슴 미어지는 비애
사랑은 분노, 철저한 증오
사랑은 통곡, 피투성이의 몸부림
사랑은 갈라섬,
일치를 향한 확연한 갈라섬
사랑은 고통, 참혹한 고통
사랑은 실천, 구체적인 실천
사랑은 노동, 지루하고 괴로운 노동자의 길
사랑은 자기를 해체하는 것,
우리가 되어 역사 속에 녹아들어 소생하는 것
사랑은 잔인한 것, 냉혹한 결단
사랑은 투쟁, 무자비한 투쟁
사랑은 회오리,
온 바다와 산과 들과 하늘이 들고일어서
폭풍치고 번개 치며 포효하여 핏빛으로 새로이 나는 것
그리하여 마침내 사랑은
고요의 빛나는 바다
햇살 쏟아지는 파아란 하늘

이슬 머금은 푸른 대지 위에
생명 있는 모든 것들 하나이 되어
춤추며 노래하는 눈부신 새날의
위대한 잉태

바람이 돌더러

모래 위에 심은 꽃은
화창한 봄날에도 피지 않는다
대나무가 웅성대는 것은
바람이 불기 때문이다
갈대가 두 손 쳐들며 아우성치는 것도
바람이 휘몰아치는 까닭이다
돌멩이가 굴러 돌사태를 일으키는 것은
바람에 제 무게를 이기지 못함이다

대나무나 갈대나 돌멩이나
바람이 불기에 소리치는 것이다

우리는 조용히 살고 싶다
돌아오는 건 낙인찍힌 해고와 배고픔
몽둥이에 철창신세뿐인 줄 빤히 알면서
소리치며 나설 자 누가 있겠느냐
그대들은 우리더러
노동문제를 일으킨다 하지만
우린 돌처럼 풀처럼 조용히 살고 싶다

다만 모래밭의 메마른 뿌리를
기름진 땅을 향해 뻗어 가야겠다
우리도 봄날엔 소박한 꽃과 향기를 피우고 싶다
우리로 하여금 소리치게 하고
돌사태를 일으키게 하는 것은
바람이 드세게 몰아쳐
더 이상 견디지 못하기 때문이다

밥을 찾아

이런 밥,
부잣집 개라면 안 먹일 거야
기계라도 덜거덕 소리가 날 거야
우리들은 식사를 거부하고
마지막 지점,
옥상으로 모였다

바람마저 자그맣게 열리어 타오르는
심장을 얼리려는 듯 차가워
기대인 어깨로 서로의 체온을 나누며
우리가 누릴 수 있는 건 굶을 자유뿐이라고
낙엽 같은 웃음으로 배를 불렸다

거치른 얼굴들이 떨며
죽순처럼 일어설 때
구둣발 소리 당당하게
번질한 얼굴들이 무겁게 내리눌러
두려운 눈과 눈 마주하며
먹구름짱 걷어낼 햇살처럼 떳떳한

우리를 확인했다

바위 같은 우리를 누가 흔들까
내 손가락 잡아먹은
톱니바퀴보다 더 힘껏 얽힌
밥 찾는 우리를 누가 가를까

사장님은 우릴 가족처럼 대한다더니
빼빼 말릴 거냐!
쟁기질하는 소도 여물을 먹여야 일하는데
이 밥을 먹고 어찌 일해요!
중도반 3년 근무에
밤마다 피기침하는 영주가 울부짖고
당신네들 건강과잉은 우리의 곯은 육신이고
행복 어린 웃음은 일그러진 좌절과 슬픔이라고
누군가가 외칠 때
오! 당신들,
미끈한 혓바닥에 이젠 더 안 속아
경찰을 부른다 해도 이젠 더 못 참아

무식한 공순이 공돌이 기업 망친다
구속시킨다 해도
이제 더는 더는 물러설 수 없어

저들의 충견들이 몽둥이를 들 때
우리의 벗들은 피투성이가 되고
핏빛이 가슴가슴 저며 들어 비겁을 녹이고
눈망울에 불꽃이 튀어 솟아
열여섯 난 명이는 무섭다 울며
수수깡 같은 몸매를 내 야윈 품으로 안겨 오고
표창장을 태우고 모범사원을 태우고
일어섰다
우뚝우뚝 일어선 우리,
밤을 지새며 노동하고 생산하는
하늘 우러러 떳떳한 노동자의 자존으로
우리 밥 찾으러,
더는 물러설 수 없는 노동자의 걸음으로
두터운 벽을 박차고 나섰다
밥을 찾으러

우리 것 찾으러
당당하게 맞서 싸우며 울부짖는
오백의 함성이 공단하늘 메아리칠 때
양처럼 순한 표정으로 사정하는
저 숨겨진 발톱을,
저 웃음 뒤의 음모를 우리는 안다

마음까지 풍성한 밥을 놓고
자꾸만 흐르는 눈물
소주잔을 돌리며
지금부터다!
굳게 잡은 손목으로
빛나는 눈동자 마주할 때
눈보라 치는
꽁꽁 얼어붙은 땅 저편으로
다사로운 봄날은
무겁게 아프게 열리고 있었다

대결

아늑한 사장실에서
책상을 마구 치며
노조를 포기하라고
개새끼들, 불순분자라고
길길이 날뛰는 저들의 머리 속은
기업주와 노동자는 사슴과 돼지처럼
결코 동등할 수 없다는
계급사상으로 굳건히 무장되어 있는지 모른다

묵묵히 일하고 시키는 대로 따르고
주는 대로 받고 성은에 감복하는 복종과 충직만이
산업평화와 안정된 사회를 이루는
훌륭한 노동자의 도리라고 생각할지 모르지만
인간이란
동등하게 존중하며 일치할 때 안정이 있고
민주적이고 평등하게 서로를 받쳐 줄 때
큰 힘이 나온다는 걸
우리는 체험으로 안다

돈과 무력과 권력을 전지전능한 하느님으로 믿는
봉건적이고 독재적인 저들과
온 세상 관계가 평등과 사랑으로 일치되어야 한다고 믿는
민주적으로 단결된 우리와의
이 팽팽한 대결

계급사상이 골수에 박힌 저들은
가진 자와 노동자는 사슴과 돼지처럼
별종으로 구분되기를 원할지 모르지만
그대들이 짓밟고 깨뜨릴수록
우린 더욱더 힘차게
인간으로
평등으로
민주주의로
통일로
솟구치는
갈수록 뜨겁게 달아오르는
이 숙명적인 대결을
어찌한단 말이냐

떠나가는 노래

어야디야
상여 같은 가슴 메고
나는 떠나네

하얀 꽃송이 촘촘한 백상여 속에
설움이 얼마, 잘린 손가락의 비명이 얼마
좀먹은 폐, 핏자욱 마르지 않은 영혼들 무거워
허청허청 어야디야
나는 떠나네

허한 눈망울로 매어달리는 벗들아
떠난다 우지 마소
우리가 만난 곳은
기름먼지 자욱한 작업장 구석
빗방울처럼 괴로워 나뒹구는
절망의 땅이어도
우리가 만나야 할 곳은
이런 곳이 아니네

우리가 나눈 것은
담배 몇 대, 철야시간 버티는 깡소주잔의 울분이어도
우리가 나눠야 할 것은 그런 것만이 아니네

늘어진 몸으로
쓴 담배연기 날릴 때
허공을 나는 새가 부러웠지

나는 한 마리 새처럼
아늑한 보금자리 찾아가는 것이 아니네

죽음의 연기 뿜어내는
저 거대한 굴뚝 속을
폭탄 품고 추락하는 새라네

어야디야
상여 같은 가슴 메고 나는 떠나네
어야디야
우리 다시 만나세

사랑 가득한
높낮이 없는 새 땅을 위하여
짓눌러진 육신,
갈라선 것들이 하나로 제 모습 찾는
싸움 속에서 다시 만나세

하얀 꽃송이 촘촘한
백상여 무거워
허청허청 울며 절며
나는 떠나네
어야디이야

떠다니냐

철새도 아닌데
뜬구름도 아닌데
일찍이 제 먹을 것 찾아
노오란 고향길 눈물 적시며
서울로 서울로 떠나왔제

철커덕 쇳소리가 귀에 익을 때쯤
세 끼 식권비와 매점 외상값 제하고 난
몇 푼 박봉이 나를 밀어
정들만 하면 시말서가 등을 떠밀어
이 공단 저 공장 떠밀려 다녔제

여기나 저기나 목메인 기름밥은 마찬가진데
한 곳에 정붙여 지긋이 있자 해도
왜 이리도 떠밀고 내차는 게 많으냐
이젠 옷가방 하나, 이불보따리 싸매 들고
벌건 대로를 죄인처럼 헤매이기엔 진절머리나,
낯설은 얼굴들과 냉대를 가슴에 안기엔
몸서리쳐지는데

또다시 떠나야 하나

눈을 들면 미소 짓는 달덩이 얼굴들
내 손때 묻은 기계를 잡고 열심히 일하고
일한 만큼 찾아들고, 사람대접 받는
그런 일터를 꿈꾸는데
아 이젠 떠날 수 없어
이젠 더 이상 떠다닐 순 없어
이리저리 뿌리째 떠밀려 다닌
지나온 세월은
지울 수 없는 상처뿐이야
설운 눈물의 밤뿐이야
곯은 육신뿐이야

또다시 나를 팽개치는
이따위 해고통지서에 꼬꾸라질 순 없어
철새도 아닌데, 뜬구름도 아닌데
이젠, 이젠 뿌리치고
내 발로 내 자릴 설 거야

당당하게 당당하게 맞서며
마땅히 찾아야 할 내 자리를 찾아서
이젠 다시 팽개쳐질 수 없는
꼬옥 마주 잡은
이 거칠고 여린,
뜨겁고 힘찬 손들을
결코 놓지 않을 거야

삼청교육대 I

서릿발 허옇게 곤두선
어둔 서울을 빠져 북방으로
완호로 씌운 군용트럭은 달리고 달려
공포에 질린 눈 숨죽인 호흡으로
앙상히 드러누운
아 3·8교!
살아 돌아올 수 있을까
살아 다시 3·8교를 건널 수 있을까
호령 소리 군화 발길질에 떨며
껍질을 벗기우고 머리털을 깎여
유격복과 통일화를 신고
얼어붙은 땅바닥을 좌로굴러 우로굴러
나는 삼청교육대 2기 5-134번이 된다

핏발 선 분노도 의리도 인정도
군홧발 개머리판에 작살나
제 한 몸 추스르지 못해 웃음 한 번 없이
깍지 끼고 땅을 기다 부러진 손가락
영하 20도의 땅바닥에서 동상 걸려 진물 흐르는 발바닥

얻어터져 성한 곳 하나 없는 마디마디
화장실에 쪼그려 앉아 벌건 피똥을 싸며
처음으로 소리죽여 흐느끼다
호루라기 집합 소리에 벌떡 일어선다

눈보라치는 연병장을 포복하며
원산폭격 쪼그려뛰기 피티체조 선착순
처지면 돌리고 쓰러지면 짓밟히고
꿈틀대면 각목으로 피투성이가 되어
내무반을 들어서면
한강철교 침상위에수류탄 철모깔고구르기
군홧발로 조인트 까져 나뒹굴고
빼치카벽에 세워 놓고 주먹질 발길질에
게거품 물고 침몰해 가는
아 여기는 강제수용소인가 생지옥인가

그렁그렁 탱크이빨에 씹히는 꿈에 소스라치면
흥건한 식은땀에 헛소리 신음 소리
흐느끼는 소리 이를 앙가는 저주 소리

그 속에서도 아직은 살아 있다는 걸 확인하고자
우리는 밤마다 조심스레 가슴을 연다

김형은 체불임금 요구하며 농성 중에
사장놈 멱살 흔들다 고발되어 잡혀 오고
열다섯 난 송군은 노가다 일 나간
어머니 마중길에 불량배로 몰려 끌려오고
딸라빚 밀려 잡혀 온 놈
시장 좌판터에서 말다툼하다 잡혀 온 놈
술 한잔 하고 고함치다 잡혀 온 놈
춤추던 파트너가 고관부인이라 잡혀 온 놈
우리는 피로와 아픔 속에서도
미칠 듯한 외로움과 공포를 휘저으며
살아야 한다고 꼭 다시
살아 나가야 한다고
얼어 터진 손과 손을 힘없이 맞잡는다

날이 갈수록 야수가 되어
헉헉거리다 탈진하여

마지막 벼랑 끝에 서서
차라리 포근한 죽음을 갈구하며
따스한 속살 내음을 그리며
단 한 순간만이라도 인간이고자
일어서 울부짖던 사람들은
무자비한 구타 속에 의무실로 실려가고
장파열 뇌진탕 질식사로
하나둘 죽어 나가
뜬눈으로 가슴 타는 초췌한 여인 앞에
돈 많이 벌어올 아빠를 기다리는 초롱한 아가 앞에
360만 원짜리 재 한 상자로 던져진다

민주노조를 몸부림치다
개처럼 끌려온 불순분자 이군은
퉁퉁 부은 다리를 절뚝이며
아버지뻘의 노약한 문노인을 돌봐 주다
야전삽에 찍혀 나가떨어지고
너무한다며 대들던 제강공장 김형도
개머리판에 작살나 앰블런스에 실려 나간다

잔업 끝난 퇴근길에 팔뚝에 새겨진 문신 하나로 잡혀 와
가슴 조이며 기다릴 눈매 선선한
동거하던 약혼녀를 자랑하며
꼭 살아 나가야 한다고 울먹이던 심형은
끝내 차디차게 식어 버리고
일제시절 징용도 이보단 덜했다며
손주 같은 군인들에게 얻어맞던 육십고개 송노인도
화통에 부들부들 뻗어 버리고
아무 죄도 없이 전과자라는 이유로 끌려왔다며
고래고래 악쓰던 사십줄 최씨는
끝내 탈영하여 백골봉에 올라
포위한 군인들과 대치하다가
분노의 폭발음으로 터져 날아가 버린다

악몽 속에 몸부림쳐도 떨치려 해도
온몸을 뒤흔들며 묻을래야 잊을래야
잊을 수 없는 80년의 겨울
개처럼 죽어간 자들의
시퍼런 원혼은 지금도 이 땅의 어드메를 떠돌고 있을까

가련한 살붙이와 여인네들은
이 휘황한 거리의 어디쯤에서 노점상으로 쫓기며
네온싸인보다 섬뜩한 원한으로 서려 있을까
그 많은 동기생들은
흐린 날이면 욱신대는 뼈마디 주무르며
지금쯤 어느 일터 어느 구석에서
삭아내리고 있을까
허연 칼날을 갈고 있을까

동상에 잘려나간 발가락의 허전함보다
철야 한 번 하고 나면 온통 쥐어뜯는
폐차 직전의 내 육신보다 더 뼈저린 지난 세월 속에
진실로 진실로
순화되어야 할 자들은
우리가 아닌 바로 저들임을,
푸르게
퍼렇게
시퍼런 원한으로
깊이깊이 못 박혀

화려한 조명으로
똑똑히 밝혀 오는
피투성이 폭력의 천지
힘없는 자의 철천지 원한
되살아나
부들부들 치떨리는
    80년 그 겨울
    삼청교육대

어머니

남도의 허기진 오뉴월 뙤약볕 아래
호미를 쥐고 밭고랑을 기던 당신 품에서
말라붙은 젖을 빨며
당신 몸으로 갈 고기 한 점 쌀밥 한 술
연하고 기름진 것을 받아먹으며
거미처럼 제 어미 몸을 파먹으며 자랐습니다

독새풀죽 쑤어 먹고 어지럼 속에 커도
못 배워 한 많은 노동자로 몸부림쳐도
도둑질은 하지 않았습니다
일 안 하고 놀고먹지도
남을 괴롭히지도 않았습니다
나로 하여 이 세상에서 단 하나
슬픔을 준 사람이 있다면
어머니 바로 당신입니다

당신의 오직 하나 소원이라면
가진 것 적어도 오손도손 평온한 가정이었지요
저는 열심히 일했고 떳떳하게 요구했고

양심대로 우리들의 새날을 위해 싸웠습니다
투쟁이 깊어 갈수록 우리에겐 풍파가 몰아쳤고
당신은 더 불안하고 체념 속에 주저앉아
다시 나를 붙들고 애원하며 원망합니다
어머니
환갑이 넘어서도 파출부살이를 하는
당신의 염원은 우리 모두의 꿈입니다
가난했기에 못 배웠기에
수모와 천대와 노동에 시퍼런 한 맺혔기에
오손도손 평온한 가정에의 바램은
마땅한 우리 모두의 비원입니다

오! 어머니
당신 속엔 우리의 적이 있습니다
어머님의 염원을
오손도손 평온한 가정에의 바램을
잔혹하게 짓밟고 선 저들은
간교하게도 당신의 비원 속에
굴종과 이기주의와 탐욕과 안일의 독사로 도사리며

간악한 적의 가장 집요하고 공고한 혓바닥으로
우리의 가장 약한 인륜을 파고들며 유혹합니다

이 세상에 태어나 단 한 사람
어머니의 가슴에 못을 박습니다
어머님의 간절한 소원을 위하여
이 땅의 모든 어머니들의 비원을 위하여
짓눌리고 빼앗긴 행복을 되찾기 위해
오늘 우리는 불효자가 되어
저 참혹한 싸움터로 울며울며
당신 곁을 떠나갑니다

어머님의 피눈물과 원한을 품고서
기필코 사랑과 효성으로 돌려드리고야 말
우리들의 소중한 평화를 쟁취하고자
피투성이 싸움 속에서
승리의 깃발을 드높이 펄럭이며 빛나는 얼굴로 돌아와
큰절 올리는 그 날까지
어머님 우리는 천하의 불효자입니다

당신 속에 도사린 적의 혓바닥을
냉혹하게 적대적으로 끊어 버리는
진실로 어머니를 사랑하옵는
천하의 몹쓸 불효자 되어
피눈물을 뿌리며 싸움터로 나아갑니다
어머니
어머니

아름다운 고백

사람들은 날보고 신세 조졌다고 한다
동료들은 날보고 걱정된다고 한다

사람들아
나는 신세 조진 것도 없네
장군이 이등병으로 강등된 것도
억대자산 부도난 것도
관직에서 쫓겨난 것도
전무에서 과장으로 좌천된 것도 아니네

아무리 해봤자 12년 묵은 기술이야 몸에 살아 있고
허고많은 일자리 중에 좀 불편하면 어떤가
까짓거 애당초 배운 것 없고 가진 것 없어 기름쟁이 되어
백 년 가라 빡빡 기어 봤자
사장이 되것는가
장관 자리 하것는가
사무직 출세하것는가
한 서너 달 감방 산들 살찌고 편하고 수양되데그랴
노동자가 언제는 별 볼일 있었나

조질 신세도 없고 찍혀 봤자 별 볼일 없네

벗들이여
너무 걱정 말게
이렇게 열심히 당당하게 살아가지 않는가
진실로 부끄러이 고백하건대
나는 이기적이고 독선적인 경쟁하는 인간이었네
내게 득이 되면 친구라 했고 손해 볼 듯하면 버렸네
동료를 불신하고 필요한 만큼만 알고 이용가치로만 따졌네
좌절과 허망 속에 그저 일하고 먹고 자고 취하고
산다는 의미조차 없이
겉멋과 향락만 동경하며 내 한 몸조차 보존키 어려웠네

노동운동을 하고부터
동료와의 깊은 신뢰와 나눔과 사랑 속에
참말 인간다운 삶이 무엇인지를 알았네
나의 존재를 인정받고 신뢰와 사랑 속에
동료를 위해 사는 것처럼 큰 희열이 어디 있을까
라면 한 개 쓴 소주 한 병을 노나 먹어도 웃음꽃이 피고

불안함과 경계가 없이 너나가 우리로 다 함께
환히 열린 하나 됨 속에서 해방의 기쁨을 나는 맛보네
나의 눈물이 동료들의 웃음이 되고
나의 고통이 동료들의 기쁨이 되고
나의 아픔이 우리들의 희망이 된다면
이 또한 얼마나 아름답고 뜻깊은 생인가

신세 조겼다 해도 좋다
이 땅의 노동형제들의 얼굴에 웃음꽃이 만발하는,
죽음 같은 저임금과 장시간 노동의 형틀을 깨부수는
노동운동의 열기 찬 대열 속에서
보람과 자랑스런 노동자로
오늘도 낯설은 현장에서
지루함과 수모도 차근차근 삭여 가며
지칠 줄 모르는 투쟁의 불꽃은 타네

별 볼일 없는 나는

얼굴도 못생기고
말주변도 어눌하고
빽도 없고 돈도 없고
최종학력 중퇴에다 촌시러워서
내 스스로 주제를 생각해 봐도
참말로 한심하게 별 볼일 없는 나는
사기는 안 친다
남의 것을 뺏지도 억누르지도
나로 인해 타인에게 슬픔은 주지 않는다

별 볼일 없는 나를
후배들은 자상한 형이라 따르고
동료들은 신의 깊은 놈이라 믿어 주고
선배들은 싸가지 있는 놈이라 인정해 준다

별 볼일 없는 나이지만
내가 없었다면
이렇게 바르게 살아가고
우리 권리 찾아 싸워 가는 좋은 벗들은

제 밑 닦기에 허둥대다
유성처럼 의미 없이 스쳐 갔을지도 모른다

그래,
니나 내나 좆도 별 볼일 없지만
우리는 흩어진 돌멩이를 모아
딴딴히 굳히는 시멘트이지

돈 가지고 빽 가지고 이론 가지고
찬란하게 인품 잡는 스타는 아니어도
우리 모두를 굳건한 단결로 엮어 세우는
굵고 썩지 않는 동아줄이지

소중하고 소중한
우리 속의 희망
끝까지 현장에서
살아 활동하는 노동자이지

장벽

내가 길들여진 노동자였을 때
저임금의 응달 속을 장시간 노동에 지쳐
캄캄한 장벽을 운명으로 알고 살아왔었다

내가 눈을 떴을 때
높고 두터운 장벽 사이로
한 줄기 빛이 내렸다

내가 외쳤을 때
내 입은 봉해졌고
메아리쳐 온 허망한 상처뿐이었다

내가 뛰어가 부딪쳤을 때
장벽은 끄떡도 하지 않았고
동료들은 차갑게 피를 닦아 주었다

내가 속삭이며,
긴 세월을 절뚝이며 속삭여
동료들과 함께 엉켜 들어

맨몸으로 수없이 벽을 쳤을 때
피에 젖은 장벽은 금이 가기 시작했다

우리가 함마로 구멍을 뚫고
긴긴 밤을 숨죽이며 다이나마이트를 터뜨렸을 때
콰르르르 거대한 장벽은 무너지고
너와 나 사이 가슴 속의 장벽도
무너져 내렸다

우리가 환히 열린 언덕으로 뛰어갔을 때
캄캄한 장벽 밑마다
쿵쿵 까부수는 소리
에워싸며 구멍 뚫는 소리
참혹한 비명 소리
우리들은 또다시 전열을 추스르며
수없이 불어난 동지들과
탄탄한 연대 위에서
마땅히 누려야 할
우리들의 평등한 푸르른 대지를 향해

너는 함마
나는 다이나마이트
살덩이로 불꽃으로 불도쟈로
갈수록 무겁고 힘찬, 치밀하고 확실한
노동자의 전진을 내어 딛는다

우리들의 숙명인
저임금과 장시간 노동이 사라질 때까지
억압과 착취와 분단의 장벽이
사라질 때까지

허깨비

내일 아침 신문에
국회가 해산되었다 해도
우린 놀라지 않는다

노총이 없어졌다 해도
우린 더 이상 슬퍼하지 않는다

밥 찾는 몸부림에 철퇴를 내리는
사법부의 판결에도 우린 더 이상 애통해하지 않는다

먹물들이 개소릴 해도
중놈, 신부, 목사란 놈들이 씨나락을 까도
언론이 물구나물 서도
우린 분노하지 않는다

우리들의 애절한 사랑,
떨리는 소망과 비원을 배신한
저 달콤한 포장을, 허깨비를
우린 더 이상 기대하지도 믿지도 않는다

그대들이 어쩔 수 없이 비춰 준 것들에
우린 만족하지 않겠다
죽음 같은 노동과 삶이,
핏발 선 싸움이 준
이 뼈저린 각성으로
마땅히 찾아야 할 우리 것을
더 이상 버려두지 않겠다
살기 좋은 이 강산은 그대들의 땅
우린 더 이상,
허깨비에 홀리지 않는다

노동하는 우리들의 땅
　　　　우리들의 내일
　　　　　우리들의 꿈으로
온 세상 하나 되어 손에 손잡는
벅찬 새날을 위하여
우리는 우릴 가로막는
저 달콤한 허깨비를
부수며 나갈 것이다

Glossary

"**Ah, Ah . . . Our Republic of Korea**" [in "Sunset" and "A Hand Grave"]: A sensational song from the 1980s glorifying the (uneven) prosperity of South Korea, first released in 1983 and sung by the popular singer Jeong Sura. On the streets lined with fully armed riot police, this song—with the line "where you can get whatever you want and achieve whatever you wish for"—could be heard daily. The song was also part of the pop music genre called "wholesome songs" (*geonjeon gayo*) promoted by the government in the 1970s and 1980s.

attending police [in "Calling for Fingerprints"]: A term referring to the ubiquitous presence of the police. The Korean term is *imseok gyeongchal*. *Imseok* means "taking a seat in an authoritative manner." At the time, the general mood was that the police were present—*imseok*—everywhere in a repressive way.

bap [in "Searching for Food" and "Illusions"]: Cooked rice or a meal. It also means "livelihood" or a "way to live" and implies the thing that provides meaning and purpose in life, not just food to relieve hunger.

bar wagon [in "The Bar Wagon" and "Bargain Sale"]: A mobile drinking stall, usually pulled by hand, where food and alcoholic beverages are sold at a low price. Operated by one or two people and parked on the street, it served the working people into the late hours. The Korean word *pojang macha* means "covered wagon." The original type is disappearing today.

bit [in "A Real Worker"]: A key tool of the lathe machine. The hard, sharp tip is used to shave and carve various metal parts. The Korean term is *baiteu*.

Bongcheondong hilltop [in "A Hand Grave"]: A hillside neighborhood in south Seoul that once included a large poor and working-class area.

coin betting [in "Where Will We Go?"]: A betting game in which coins are tossed inside clasped hands and divided into two fists. The Korean term is *jjaljjari*. The betting player guesses whether the coins in each hand are odd or even in number. This simple type of gambling was especially popular among the underprivileged and working people.

donghoe [in "Calling for Fingerprints"]: The local government office. A less used, old term for *dongsamuso*, meaning "neighborhood administrative office" (*dong* is the administrative unit "neighborhood").

Duman River, Oryuk Islands, Forsythia Girl, Bakdal Pass [in "The Bar Wagon"]: References to popular songs in the second half of the twentieth century in South Korea. Singing such songs was part of the drinking culture at the time. The specific songs are "Duman River Full of Tears" ("Nunmuljeojeun Dumangang"), "Please Return to Busan Harbor" ("Dorawayo Busanhange"), "Forsythia Girl" ("Gaenari Cheonyeo"), and "Crossing the Bakdal Pass While Crying" ("Ulgoneomneun Bakdaljae"), respectively.

Eunhasu [in "A Hand Grave"]: The name of a popular cigarette brand in the 1980s, first released in 1978. The name means "The Milky Way."

factory girl, factory boy [in "Made for Each Other," "Garibong Market," "English Conversation," and "Searching for Food"]: Somewhat derogatory terms for young women and men who work at factories. The Korean terms are *gongsuni* and *gongdori*, respectively. Many factory workers at the time stopped attending school and started work in their teens due to unfavorable economic situations.

fatherland of progress [in "Working on Sunday" and "A Hand Grave"]: A common slogan of the Chun Doo-Hwan government, an entity that deployed much political repression. The Korean term is *seonjinjoguk*. Many people at the time spoke about *seonjinjoguk* in an ironic way.

Five-Eight-Eight District [in "Made for Each Other"]: A former red-light district in northeast Seoul, between the neighborhoods of Cheongnyangnidong and Jeonnongdong. The name Five-Eight-Eight refers to a street number in the district. The Korean term is *Opalpal*.

Garibong Factory District [in "Calling for Fingerprints"]: A large industrial area in the neighborhood of Garibongdong (*dong* is the administrative unit "neighborhood"). Also part of Guro Gongdan. Established in 1964 to manufacture goods mainly for export, it employed around a hundred thousand workers in the 1980s.

Garibong Market [in "Garibong Market"]: A vibrant semi-outdoor market in the district of Guro in southwest Seoul, named after the neighborhood it is in, Garibongdong. The market, with its many small shops and restaurants, originally served the working people in the area.

gimbap [in "Garibong Market"]: A food item of rice rolled in flattened laver seaweed. It often has vegetables and meat inside. It is considered fast food that is affordable and ubiquitous. Also, it represents casual outdoor dining. The word means "seaweed rice."

Granada, Royale Salon, Stella, Titan [in "A Hand Grave"]: Names of automobiles in South Korea at the time. They are Hyundai Granada, Daewoo Royale Salon, Hyundai Stella, and Kia Titan, respectively. The automobiles are mentioned in the poem in the order of decreasing luxuriousness, the Granada being the most expensive sedan and the Titan truck being the least hospitable for passengers.

grease meal [in "Off to Rot," "Bargain Sale," and "Am I Drifting?"]: A term signifying factory labor. The Korean term is *gireumbap*, literally "grease meal." The life of a factory worker was described as "eating the grease meal" (*gireumbap meongneunda*), because these workers made a living by getting their bodies and clothing soiled with grease and oils.

greaser [in "The Bar Wagon" and "A Beautiful Confession"]: A person who works with machines and is thus exposed to the oils and grease needed to operate them. The term also refers to factory workers in general. The Korean term is *gireum jaengi*.

hanja [in "Where Will We Go?" and "Sunset"]: Korean-language vocabulary written with sinographic characters (Chinese characters). Until recently, mastering thousands of characters was a marker of a learned person, as sinographs were commonly used in newspapers and books. Many working people in the 1980s, who did not have much formal education, studied hanja on their own or at night schools, along with English. Even today, learning hundreds of sinographic characters is useful for a well-rounded life.

Han River [in "The Han River"]: A major river in South Korea that runs east to west through Seoul. The Korean name is Hangang. The river begins in Gangwon Province and flows into the Yellow Sea. It was a symbol of South Korea's industrialization, as in the phrase "the miracle on the Han River." At the same time, the severe level of pollution of the river was an indication of industrialization's numerous problems.

Han River human bridge, grenade-on-the-bed, helmet roll [in "Samcheong Reeducation Camp I"]: Harsh military drills commonly exercised prior to the period of democratization, in the late 1980s. Such drills were exercised not only at military bases but also at schools and reeducation camps like Samcheong.

Italian towel [in "The Bar Wagon"]: A scrubbing towel with a coarse surface used during bathing. The Korean term is *itaeri taol*. The word literally means "Italian towel." One origin story is that an imported fabric from Italy was so coarse that it was marketed as an exfoliating bath towel.

jjajangmyeon [in "Made for Each Other"]: A noodle dish made with fermented black bean paste. This dish is Chinese in origin and was reinvented by Chinese Koreans in the early twentieth century in Korea's Chinatowns. In Korean food culture, jjajangmyeon is an affordable and delicious dish for dining out, enjoyed by all.

jjambap [in "Off to Rot" and "Dawn of Labor"]: Meals prepared at military bases. In the past, these meals were of low quality. The word derives from the term *janban*, which means "leftover food," indicating poor quality. A secondary meaning is "life experience" gained from the military, schools, jobs, and other often-hierarchical organizations, with the implication of surviving in difficult settings. A person who has eaten a lot of jjambap has gone through the challenges of an organizational life.

Jongno [in "Made for Each Other" and "A Hand Grave"]: A district in central Seoul. For centuries, Jongno has been a center of commerce, culture, and leisure for all groups of people.

Kentucky chicken [in "Garibong Market" and "Maybe"]: Fried chicken. The name derives from the U.S. restaurant chain Kentucky Fried Chicken. Before it became widely produced in South Korea, fried chicken was often called "Kentucky chicken." In traditional Korean cuisine, chicken is never fried whole. The name entered the Korean lexicon through U.S. military bases before the chain opened in South Korea.

labor office [in "The Bar Wagon"]: The unit in a company involved in managing the welfare of the workers. The Korean term for the head of labor relations is *nomu gwajang*. At the time, this person carried out the task of stopping various disputes in advance. *Nomu gwajang* was a symbol of the oppressive workspace in the 1980s, when the workers were controlled by various mechanisms to prevent confrontation between workers and owners.

makgeolli [in "The Bar Wagon"]: Unfiltered rice wine that is about 6 percent alcohol. Along with soju, it is an affordable drink and thus enjoyed by the working people.

night school [in "Maybe"]: A nighttime learning institution for workers who had to earn money during the day for survival and therefore could not attend regular school. Often, these night schools were preparatory schools for various licenses and certificates.

pechka stove [in "Samcheong Reeducation Camp"]: A large fireplace and cooking stove set into the wall of a room, often built in South Korea's military bases. The name comes from the traditional Russian stove.

peeling the back layer [in "Calling for Fingerprints"]: People who received their South Korean registration cards before the year 2000, when the photo became digital, know this procedure. The thin back layer of one's identification photo is peeled, so that the slightly coarse surface would better allow the photo to be glued on the card.

polishing team [in "Searching for Food"]: A team responsible for sanding and polishing the surface of goods like electric guitars and pianos. The Korean term is *jungdoban*. This team worked in a constant cloud of harmful dust.

press [in "Heaven," "Sleepiness," and "A Hand Grave"]: Machines that change the shape of the raw material by pressure. The Korean term is *peureseu*. All factories needing the compression of raw materials would have a press machine. At the time, many workers whose job was to insert the raw material under the press machine had poor concentration due to exhaustion and lost their fingers or hands.

QC activities [in "English Conversation"]: Activities related to quality control (QC) at production sites. However, in the name of improvement, QC activities were often used to increase labor intensity. Workers at the time regularly talked about how much they hated QC activities.

ramyeon [in "No Other Way" and "A Beautiful Confession"]: Instant noodles sold in plastic packs, consumed in South Korea since 1963. The term literally means "boiled noodles." The affordability and good flavor of ramyeon—as well as its marketing—enabled it to become a staple for students and working people. Consuming ramyeon with soju was—and still is—a way of eating and drinking on the cheap. Today ramyeon is enjoyed by nearly everyone in South Korea.

Samcheong Reeducation Camp [in "Samcheong Reeducation Camp I"]: An extralegal detention camp established by the Chun Doo-Hwan government (1980–1988). On August 4, 1980, the Chun regime announced the "Special Measure to Eradicate Social Ills and Decree of Martial Law Number 13," for the purpose of "refining and educating" those who were perceived as criminals and violators of public morals and decency. Training facilities were set up at military bases, and the detained people faced systematic violence. According to the military and the police, over sixty thousand people were arrested without warrants and sent to the camp. The Ministry of Defense at the time reported that fifty-seven people died at the camps, but during the Roh Tae-Woo regime, an additional four hundred deaths were officially recorded. In 2003, a law on reparations was enacted.

savings club [in "Sleepiness" and "Working on Sunday"]: A traditional money savings club that operates outside the official banking system. The Korean term is *gye*. The members of the club contribute a certain amount every month. The total monthly amount is then collected each month by a different member on a rotating basis. For instance, if a savings club has twelve members, then each member will collect the total monthly amount once every twelve months.

sida [in "Garibong Market," "Record of My Journey with Men," "The Dream of an Apprentice," "Sleepiness," and "Sunset"]: An apprentice. A person new to a job who assists a skilled worker. It comes from the Japanese word meaning "below" (*shita*). The term describes an unskilled worker who labors without much privilege.

soju [in "Where Will We Go?," "The Bar Wagon," "Off to Rot," "Bargain Sale," "A Hand Grave," "Dawn of Labor," "No Other Way," "Searching for Food," "A Song about Leaving," and "A Beautiful Confession"]: A popular Korean beverage that is 20 to 40 percent alcohol. The name literally means "burned spirit." Soju comes in two forms. One is the distilled version made from rice, potatoes, sweet potatoes, or grains, which has a higher price. The other is the lower-priced version made for mass consumption, which is typically packaged in a green bottle. This type of soju is a mixture of drinkable ethanol, water, and flavoring. Because of its low price (cheaper than beer), soju has been the preferred alcoholic beverage of the working class. It is also a drink that symbolizes the struggle of and solidarity among workers.

start early, end late [in "Where Will We Go?" and "A Real Worker"]: The notion of going to work early in the morning and leaving work late at night, commonly expressed and demanded by owners and managers during the time, as if it would boost the workers' morale. The Korean term is *jochul cheorya*.

sundae [in "Garibong Market"]: A type of sausage made by stuffing meat, vegetables, grains, noodles, and pig's blood into pig intestines. At the time, sundae was considered an affordable meat item for the working people. It is a widely enjoyed dish today.

Taiming [in "The Dream of an Apprentice"]: A brand of wake-up pills taken by workers to get them through the night shift. The pills were readily provided by the factories. The name derives from the English word "timing."

Three-Eight Bridge [in "Samcheong Reeducation Camp I"]: A bridge in the city of Pocheon, forty kilometers north of Seoul (about twenty-five miles). The Korean name is Sampalgyo. The name refers to the division at the thirty-eighth parallel. This bridge leads to the so-called frontline of South Korea, the border region close to North Korea. Soldiers and detainees crossing this bridge at the time felt the tension and isolation of the area.

Toad [in "The Bar Wagon"]: The logo of the Jinro soju company is the toad. The Korean term is *dukkeobi*. At the time, customers at drinking establishments would order soju by saying, "One bottle of Toad, please."

tongbak [in "Becoming Wise"]: A kind of wisdom gained from harsh experience, similar to street smarts. The word also signifies the human head.

Tongil Boots [in "Samcheong Reeducation Camp I"]: The name of government-issued ankle-high boots given to soldiers and reserves in the 1970s. The name means "unification boots." They were made from rubber and canvas, to save cost.

ttallabit [in "Samcheong Reeducation Camp I"]: A private underground loan with a high interest. The word means "dollar debt." It originates from the postwar period in South Korea, when loan sharks used the U.S. dollar as standard currency.

tteokbokki [in "Garibong Market"]: An affordable dish of rice or flour cake stewed in a spicy red-pepper sauce. It started as street food popular among students and young workers but is now consumed widely. The word means "stir-cooked cake."

Union Federation [in "Illusions"]: A shortened name of the pro-government union group, the Federation of Korean Trade Unions. The abridged Korean term is Nochong. At the time, the Union Federation was an organization that regularly suppressed the labor movement and acted against the interest of the workers. Naturally, the Union Federation was a target of workers' protests.

washing greasy clothes [in "No Other Way"]: The daily chore of washing work clothes that have been soiled with oil and grease. The Korean term is *gireum ppallae*.

where you can get whatever you want and achieve whatever you wish for [in "A Hand Grave"]: A well-known lyric from the song "Ah, Ah . . . Our Republic of Korea," which was a government-endorsed song about the sensational development of South Korea. *See also* **"Ah, Ah . . . Our Republic of Korea."**

winter of '80 [in "Samcheong Reeducation Camp I"]: The winter of 1980 was bleak. After Chun Doo-Hwan's military takeover in December 1979 and the Gwangju Uprising in

May 1980, many people who were detained to receive "societal refinement" ended up dead.

won [in "How much?," "Where Will We Go?," "The Bar Wagon," "Garibong Market," "Record of My Journey with Men," "Bargain Sale," "Working on Sunday," "A Hand Grave," and "Samcheong Reeducation Camp I"]: The name of the currency in the two Koreas. In 1984 in South Korea, 1,000 won was US$1.25 (1 million won = US$1,250). A factory worker at the time made between 4,000 and 5,000 won per day (between US$5.00 and US$6.25 per day). A plate of sundae was 300 won or US$0.38.

Wonsan bombing stance [in "Samcheong Reeducation Camp I"]: A painful drill of endurance in which a tripod stance is formed with the top of the head planted on the ground, hands clasped on the lower back, waist bent, and legs straight. The head is to resemble a bomb hitting the ground. Wonsan is a port city in the east of North Korea that was heavily bombed during the Korean War.

The Worker-Poet in Mass Culture

Janet Poole

When *Dawn of Labor* was published in 1984, the government ban could not stem the reading public's urgent desire for Park Nohae's first collection of poems. The collection sold quickly and amassed sales of nearly one million copies. For poets and their readers around the world, and even in South Korea today, the idea of a small poetry book selling one million copies seems outlandish. But in 1980s South Korea, the popularity of this genre of writing was not unusual. I recall my astonishment when, four years after Park's debut appeared, I walked into a bookstore in Seoul only to be overwhelmed by piles of poetry books near the doorway. In the bustle of a crowded downtown bookstore, the poetry collections seemed to tumble off the displays into readers' hands. It was clear that poetry was selling, but I instantly wondered, why poetry? What did poetry summon up that appealed to such large masses of readers? Surely it was communicating something of urgency, something that resonated. What's more, among those tumbling volumes, Park's book was falling into readers' hands more frequently than others. Why Park Nohae's poetry?

Park Nohae became South Korea's most renowned "worker-poet" during the country's industrializing era. A laborer who had moved to the capital of Seoul at the age of sixteen and attended night school had, barely a decade later, published his first collection of poems, and it was outselling the works of established writers. In a society that already treasured poetic forms to a degree rarely matched elsewhere, a worker had now appeared and touched the heart and soul of the reading nation. The collection itself is compact: forty-two poems arranged in three sections. Park had already begun to publish some of these poems the previous year and attracted attention. The poems gathered in *Dawn of Labor* describe the rhythms of daily work experienced by the millions of laborers staffing the factories that drove South Korea's manufacturing and heavy industries. The work conditions described were excruciating, although all too widely shared and known: pay so low that feeding families was a struggle; the physical and mental exhaustion of constant mandatory overtime justified by overseas demands and deadlines, which dictated the production schedule—rather than the workers' own capacities; safety standards that led to frequent injuries, even death; and violent suppression, by both the state and corporations, of workers' attempts to organize and campaign for a more humane working life. Once curated as a collection, the poems themselves garner additional force, suggested even by the titles of the three sections: "Our Love, Our Unrelenting Life," "Dawn of Labor," and "For a New Land." The poems incubate a driving energy that is not satisfied by merely describing the present but that reaches toward a different future, a new land. As the titular poem illustrates, Park's poems herald some kind of beginning. Although that poem itself opens with a worker returning home at dawn after completing a night shift—the end of a workday—the dawn, as we all know, also presages a new day and the potential for change to come.

That change could not come soon enough for the masses of workers whose bodies literally fueled South Korea's industrial growth. By the 1980s, millions of workers were toiling in substandard conditions for substandard wages, their suffering submerged under the slogan of the "miracle on the Han River." But South Korea's economic "miracle" was far from magical for those who produced it. The experienced worker in "Bargain Sale" earns four thousand won a day (about five U.S. dollars), which, as the critic Do Jeongil has pointed out, was enough to purchase a single movie ticket at the time. Failing to find work at even that pay, the poem's speaker then proposes his own bargain sale: three thousand won, but you'll have to "buy my sorrow, my despair, and my anger, too!" A female factory worker at the time might have earned enough per day to purchase one cup of coffee. Then there was the extreme violence inflicted upon those who dared to demand a more humane life. "Samcheong Reeducation Camp I" recounts the abuse perpetrated at the camps set up by the Chun Doo-Hwan military regime for those who—for any number of reasons, ranging from organizing labor, demanding unpaid wages, or simply getting caught up in a fight at a market—were deemed in need of ideological training by the state. Such are the daily lives described so memorably in Park's poems.

Yet, Park's poems also attest to the emergence of something dynamic and creative in the midst of the climate of suppression. By the mid-1980s, a vibrant and pervasive workers' culture was fully brewing, encouraged by both formal and informal labor organizations and a seemingly insatiable desire for learning from the masses of workers, many of whom had congregated in South Korea's burgeoning cities. Literature had a particular role to play here, and it was not at all unusual to find workers gathering in the evening to discuss a recently published novel, studying foreign languages together, or writing their own poetry. Some of these study groups took on a more organized, regional, and ultimately national dimension, and some were more formalized into night schools, which might be run by student activists or even sponsored by factories. As a result, from the 1970s on, a lively production of workers' literature had emerged—mostly in the genres of poetry or personal memoir—and this creative work found venues for wider publication in journals, in union newsletters (where unions were allowed), and occasionally in book form.

Park Nohae had himself traveled to Seoul at the age of sixteen from rural South Jeolla Province. The Jeolla provinces to the southwest of the peninsula were historically agrarian, due to their fertile soil, but also impoverished by the standards of all economic markers as well as politically marginalized. Treated as a grain basin to supply the empire with rice during the Japanese colonial period, the Jeolla provinces had seen the advent of plantations, high rates of absentee landlords, and the intense polarization of wealth. In the postliberation era, the political and economic marginalization of the Jeolla provinces had only increased as President Park Chung Hee's high-speed, state-led industrialization policies had favored his own political base and hometown in the Gyeongsang provinces to the southeast. Industrialization around the capital and in the southeast had led to large-scale outmigration from the southwest, as young people and families searched for opportunities elsewhere. This is where Park Nohae had grown up, near the southern coast, not too far from the provincial capital of Gwangju, where infamously, in 1980, a political uprising was violently suppressed by government forces when the army moved in to overwhelm the citizens' occupation of a civic space, which led to the deaths of perhaps thousands of citizens. If Park, born in 1957, had left the area before the 1980 Gwangju Uprising, he was at the very least steeped in a local history that could not but provoke critique and awareness of as well as doubt about the state and the state's treatment of its own citizens. As one among millions of rural youths who migrated to urban centers in search of work and a better future, driven by necessity, Park also attended night school and began to write poetry.

It would be misleading to suggest that Park Nohae's work was the inaugural appearance of poetry dedicated to the revelation and arousal of workers. Such poetry had existed long before the rise of the worker-poet in the 1970s. Throughout the colonial era (1910–1945), a vibrant proletarian arts movement had sought to depict the abuse suffered by those working in poor conditions—both on farms in a still predominantly agrarian society and in newly emerging modern factories. The poetry of proletarian artists aimed to raise awareness among the nonlaboring classes but also to encourage solidarity among the workers themselves. However, due to small circulation numbers and low literacy levels, such poetry appeared as an avant-garde, produced by intellectuals appalled by conditions they themselves had rarely experienced directly. That avant-garde was resolutely anti-colonial and strove to unite a disparate population in the face of the ongoing absorption of Korean labor into the global capitalist regime. It is important to understand Park's oeuvre as part of this longer imbrication of art and anti-capitalist politics; indeed, we can even detect rhetorical flourishes, poetic figures and forms that seem to connect Park's work to this earlier tradition.

At the same time, what was distinct about the appearance of *Dawn of Labor* was the figure of the poet himself as the worker: the manner in which his life as a worker and his work as a poet are inseparable. He is no avant-garde leader but hails from the midst of the masses. To be sure, with the appearance of this collection, Park rose above the surface of that collective, and that rising, although celebrated, was fraught with personal danger. Searching for some degree of anonymity, he adopted the pen name Nohae, which literally means "liberation of workers." He became known as "the faceless poet" and, in the late 1980s, engaged in radical underground activism as the cofounder of the South Korean Socialist Workers' Alliance. In 1991, for his radical writing and activism with the alliance, he was arrested, tortured, faced calls for the death penalty, and sentenced to life imprisonment. Before his release from prison in 1998, he published a second volume of poems and a collection of essays, joining another tradition of poets and thinkers: those anti-colonial and anti-imperial poets writing from within the space of the prison. But in his earlier poetry, translated here, he is the worker-poet whose art seems to align more closely to life with a kind of immediacy that seems less ideological but rather imbued with simple truths, thus revealing, paradoxically, the inseparability of ideology from life itself.

The distinctive phenomenon of this worker-poet's oeuvre was, of course, its mass character. Whereas those earlier proletarian poets had presaged the future of labor and its degradations as capitalism deepened, Park's work refracted an already mass experience. This is surely why his poetry resonated with many and became a bestseller. If Korean readers were already used to approaching their most intimate thoughts through verse, then the stories recorded here—the rhythm of the overseas contract, its promise of work and the dictation of that work from a distance, and the overwhelming frequency of involuntary overtime rendering the notion of the working day opaque—were ubiquitous mass experiences, the daily lives of millions. Global capitalism inaugurates a specific temporality of labor; poetry was better placed to describe this temporality and rhythms than the long-form novel. Its abbreviated, easily reproducible forms could capture the repetitive experience of urban workers forced to commodify themselves in order to produce the increasing range of commodities deemed vital to contemporary life. It is hard not to connect the magnitude of sales of Park's poems to those mass-produced objects assembled in factories. Rather than herald Park's poems as paeans to individual genius, I believe that their creative and poetic strength emerges from the symbiosis between the masses of workers, of products, and of readers. What Park's poetry achieved that the masses of other products could not was to highlight the human character of everyday industrial work and call for its transformation. Park's poems bear witness, raise collective awareness, and call attention to the relentless cruelty of the industrial regime. They also highlight connections and shared emotions. These individual poems are transformed into a collection precisely by this rhythm of repetition, which mimics the rhythm of daily working life. Even the moments of leisure—the warm descriptions of evenings spent drinking with colleagues or staying home with family—are defined by the working day, that is, by the inability of the worker to protect the nonworking portion of the day from the excruciating demands of the global capitalist market and its uneven productions.

Vitally, poems can be easily published in different venues due to their short, fragmented nature. Poems are easily reproducible, but by no means lesser in meaning and significance on account of that. On the contrary, their reproduction only enhances their significance. By appearing here again, in English translation, Park Nohae's poems can once more call attention to harsh working conditions that, for so many workers around the world, still belong to the present and not the past, including that of today's South Korea. The translation of such immediacy is a far more challenging task than is at first apparent, and Brother Anthony of Taizé and labor historian Cheehyung Harrison Kim are to be congratulated for bringing this collection into the English language with such concrete poise. The impact of simple truth is in some ways less translatable than the most complex winding phrase—the content overwhelms. And who could not be shocked by the living and working conditions described in these pages? No complex phrasing, images, or opaque language is necessary to enhance the poetic force of the writing to move its reader; indeed, it would only distract and obscure.

What does it mean to read Park Nohae's poetry today, in the twenty-first century? And to read it in English? Reading at this historical distance, we have knowledge of Park's future. He cannot help but appear to us today as a heroic individual, his anonymity removed, the death sentence averted. The appearance of this first English translation of *Dawn of Labor*, the book that set Park on his way as perhaps the most significant worker-poet of late twentieth-century South Korea, will allow a new generation of readers around the world to discover his work. The University of Hawai'i Press, too, is to be commended for seeing this project to publication. Park's biography is compelling, but the poems should be even more so. They are not just a historical witness to the past, though viscerally they are, but also a testament to an ongoing present in which global contracts continue to drive workers' abilities to feed their families, to take overtime or not, or to live a humane life. Over the past decade, Park's work, particularly as a photographer, has explored situations of oppression and abuse throughout the world. Park Nohae has sought to shine a light on connections rather than claim exceptional conditions. The systemic abuses recorded in his poetry stemmed from a global system, and those abuses do not simply belong to the past. We should read his poems, then, less as a historical document than as part of an ongoing conversation and struggle. The dream of a new land continues, as does the struggle.

Poet Militant, Poet Inspirational

Brother Anthony of Taizé

In 1984, nobody knew who Park Nohae was. Nobody knew what he looked like, where he lived, where he worked. Nobody knew his real name. Park Nohae? Who on earth was he? All anyone knew was that he was a factory worker and a poet whose writings denounced the exploitation of industrial workers and expressed his dreams of a better world for Korea's workforce. In the South Korea of the mid-1980s, two groups of people were fascinated by him. The first group was composed of the students, dissidents, activists, and workers who were protesting the way Korean society was operating under the military dictatorship of Chun Doo-hwan, who had seized power after the assassination of the previous dictator, Park Chung Hee. The other group was the police and the Agency for National Security Planning, previously known as "the Korean CIA." The former longed to hail him face-to-face, carry him on their shoulders through the streets as a hero-poet; the latter had only one aim: to arrest him, beat him up, and put him behind bars. Nothing upsets a country's security forces like an anonymous dissident poet. Everyone knew Park Nohae's name was a pseudonym: *No* for *nodongja* (worker) and *hae* for *haebang* (liberation). He was truly a nameless poet—and a faceless one, too, since almost nobody had knowingly seen him.

Censorship could not prevent the publication in 1984 of the first collection of his poems, *Nodongui saebyeok* (*Dawn of Labor*). It was a bombshell, something totally new. There had been dissident poets before him, of course, in the 1960s and 1970s. Shin

Gyeong-nim had been one of the first, writing about the anguished lives of poverty-stricken farmers in *Farmers' Dance*. Ko Un had read stirring poems at the start of many protests throughout the 1970s and beyond. Kim Chiha had spent long years in prison for his dazzling satire of social corruption, *Five Bandits*, and had become an internationally known cause célèbre. But here was a real worker, at grips with the daily agony of workers, who could write powerful poetry! It was unheard of! In the years that followed, book sales soared, ultimately nearing a million copies. Every Korean student read Park's book. The police were on the highest alert, though in vain.

In *Dawn of Labor*, poem after poem gives voice to the voiceless workers surrounding the poet in his daily life. They simply express their feelings, caught as they are in a system where the wealthy factory owners have complete power over those they employ for a pittance. Exhaustion, poverty, lack of free time, the threat of unemployment, and the daily grind of working life are brought alive in a muted way, suiting the gravity of the situation. The opening poem expresses many of the volume's main themes:

> The rope of survival for my family of three is held by my
>   boss,
> so he's my heaven.
>
> When I am at the hospital cradling a hand crushed in the
>   press,
> the doctor can patch me up or leave me crippled,
> so he's my heaven.
>
> When we are dragged to the police for organizing a union
> after two months without pay,
> the officer who threatens to lock us up,
> though we've committed no crime,
> is always a frightening heaven.

The judges and lawyers,
who can turn us into criminals or set us free,
are a dreadful heaven.

The bureaucrats, sitting in government offices,
who can make us or break us,
are a fearsome heaven.

People high up, people with power, people with money
all appear to be heaven.
No, they are indeed heaven,
the heaven of darkness controlling our lives.

Will I ever be heaven
for someone somewhere?
I have lived only at the bottom, powerless.
But for one person,
our insanely beautiful baby,
who now begins to walk,
I may be a small, unsteady heaven.

We, too, want to become heaven.
Not a dark clouded heaven
that presses down,
but a clear blue heaven
over a world where we lift one another.

Many of the poems express bitterness and sorrow, the frustration of young working couples who almost never have time to be together, or the pain of having a day off but being too poor to go anywhere or do anything. Yet sometimes a flash of humor shines through, as when a group of workers go to renew their residence registrations, which involves having their fingerprints taken, only to discover that their fingers have been so corroded by industrial chemicals that they have no fingerprints left to give, just as they have virtually no identity in society.

Naturally, some people knew who the poet was and where he was (by then) hiding. None betrayed him. In Park Nohae's view, the challenges facing Korea's workers were essentially communal. Obviously, individuals were powerless alone. Union activities sometimes existed, but they were limited to individual factories, where it was easy to identify leaders and have them fired or arrested. Park Nohae was in close contact with groups of people who saw the need for a much broader social and political solution—a collective, revolutionary solution. Since the Korean War, and even before it began, in South Korea the word "socialist" meant "communist," the word "communist" meant "commie bastard," and for tens of thousands of innocent people, that label had been enough to result in their brutal deaths without trial or appeal. In 1989, with a new military president installed, Roh Tae-Woo, but with increasing recognition of the need for a return to purely civilian, democratic government, Park Nohae and a group of fellow radical activists launched the South Korean Socialist Workers' Alliance. Socialist? The South Korean security forces were put on red alert. Arrests followed. But it was only on March 10, 1991, that Park Nohae was arrested. By that time, he probably felt that his life underground, constantly on the run, had served its purpose. His true name became known—Park Gi-pyeong—and he was finally caught.

The Korean system of justice treated him as it felt a poet of his standing deserved to be treated. He was taken to a notorious building on the slopes of Seoul's Namsan, where the Korean intelligence agency had for decades tortured, and sometimes killed, its victims. There, in an underground chamber, he was tortured as much as the age now allowed. For twenty-four days and nights, he was subjected to physical and mental violence. To survive, he clung to the thought, "Just one day more! One day more! I've survived this far, surely today's my end, the last day of my life. So just this one more day, today! One more day, until my last minute, and death!" His tormentors were intent on discovering the full extent of his activist network. He knew that if he ever began to yield, they would demand another name, then another, so he kept silent. At the end of those twenty-four brutal days, he was finally produced to public view on his way to court. For the first time, the faceless poet's face was revealed, and, to the stupefaction of those who knew what he had just endured, he was smiling broadly, joyfully, on television screens and in photos published in all the newspapers.

Once his trial began, the justice system paid him the highest tribute a poet can receive. The prosecution accused him of being "an enemy of the state" and demanded the death sentence. Certainly, insofar as the South Korean state was complicit in the oppression and exploitation of millions of workers—humble, helpless citizens—Park Nohae was an enemy of the state. In the end, the sentence given was a slightly milder one: life imprisonment. He was taken to a prison in Gyeongju, in the far southeast of the country, and he began his life in solitary confinement in a tiny, unheated cell. For most prisoners placed in solitary confinement, the discomfort and loneliness soon become intolerable. For Park, they were a gift. Sentenced in 1991, by 1993 he had published a collection of poems written in prison, *Chamdoin sijak* (*True Beginning*). It sold thirty thousand copies in the first month, sixty thousand in the first year. These poems about his arrest, torture, trial, and imprisonment are a far cry from the poems about life as a worker. They are a record of near collapse, a recognition of failure, of inner and outer torment, but they are also a message of hope, a celebration of survival. The poem "The Winter Tree That Year" is the most prominent example of that:

1
Winter that year was pallid.
People hunched critical shoulders or suffered death,
  bodies quaking, they said either "Not now," or again, now
    again,

"That blue dream will not return."
The bitter north wind blowing from Moscow shook the world
as it bore away in a flash once-fluttering leaves, birds, and songs, too.
From the ashen sky, flocks of crows swooped down as if to arrest me,
binding my weary body with merciless cords.
In winter that year,
my beginning was my defeat.
[. . .]

3
Nobody could say when the winter would end.
Haggard faces, seeming dead, sick with self-criticism,
knew full well that there was nowhere, nowhere they could stand secure.
Thickening the joints and increasing the growth rings, the root raised the red frozen hands and nurtured—
produced—the moist light for itself.
Only the green, rising within its blood and bone, was its faith that winter.
A worm of desire came down, crept into the ropes binding its waist,
and finally the winter tree plucked off the ropes holding it,
coughed deeply and blazed up.
A biting night wind raged, and all through the winter,
only an aching silence reverberated like a bell within.
All kept silent but believed for sure that that long silence
was the first step toward a new birth.
In winter that year,
my defeat was my true beginning.

In the following years, Park Nohae turned his imprisonment into a process for spiritual discipline and growth. He shaved his head, rarely spoke, and wrote nothing except the poems that arose in the silence. For hours each day, he would sit, facing the wall, like a Buddhist practitioner of Zen ("Seon" in Korean). While in the outside world South Korea's social evolutions continued and the first civilian president was sworn in early 1993—a symbolic step toward the long-hoped-for democracy—Park Nohae remained in prison. In 1997, he published another collection of poems at the same time as a campaign was being organized for his release. *Sarammani huimangida* (*Only a Person Is Hope*) is a collection of poetic essays on the themes that had preoccupied Park during his years of silence. The collection starts with an account of a chance conversation between Park, on his way to prison after sentencing, and a simple worker on her way to be released. The woman recognizes him and starts to express her inmost thoughts about social activism:

> I hope for a good world, but honestly speaking, I want it
> for free.
> A good world, a good world, I say,
> but I am jealous of the riches and abilities of the wealthy.
> I've lived by stealing our children's future,
> stealing the happiness that is due to those who make
> sacrifices for a better world.
> [. . .]
> With no attempt to be a good person first,
> with no concrete action to participate and support
> by sharing out my little money, time, and attention,
> how can I hope for a better future, and for whom?
> The good world is, in some ways, already growing inside
> us.
> [. . .]
>
> With whose strength and over what length of time
> can such a good society be established?
> When will we selfish workers and ordinary people

ever change into mature adults?
Faced with her naive question
I crumbled completely.
Faced with this one woman, who lives by the diligent sweat of her brow,
faced with the question she asked from the depths of her life,
faced with her stern question, dropping on me like a ton of bricks,
ah, I lay helpless, crumbling, broken.
[. . .]

All through the past seven years, I have experienced death behind these walls.
Finding out "why I should go on living" as a failed revolutionary
was a desperate challenge. It was dreadful.
The riddle that woman gave me that evening required me
to be honest, even if it killed me, to take responsibility for the result,
it demanded a life of aching silence in which I stopped writing, shaved my head,
a life of self-discipline.
And now, after much time has passed,
I hear within me the sprouting of fresh buds.
At last, quiet hope.
The fact that I have survived and did not die,
that is my hope.
Until the day when I can stand with confidence
before the woman whom heaven sent me that evening,
my waiting and self-discipline will continue.

The entire collection is an attempt to express in verse the kind of life required if the world is to become a better, more just, more human place. Then, in 1998, a democrat, Kim Dae-Jung, became the new president of Korea. On August 15 that year, Park Nohae was amnestied and emerged from over seven years of solitary confinement.

Once Park Nohae had reestablished contact with those who had been his companions before, and with those new companions who had been deeply moved by the two prison collections, he put into practice the most important notion his reading in prison had confirmed. Nothing was more important, he felt, nothing more truly human, than community, the community that arises when people live and share together. One essential source for this vision was his experience of rural village life in his childhood, the farming community where all shared the burdens, the sorrows, and the joys of a life deeply rooted in nature. In 2000, he established a nongovernmental organization named Nanum Munhwa (Culture of Sharing), bringing together people thinking along the lines he had laid down, aimed at social transformation. Refusing financial support from the government or business conglomerates, the organization was self-sufficient, financed through member-paid dues, because only then could it retain its freedom of action.

The most striking transformation for many, however, was the poet's shift from Korean social issues to global issues. He made headlines in 2003, when the United States invaded Iraq, by going alone to Iraq to be with the children weeping in terror because of the war, part of a human shield to protect civilians and promote peace. In 2006, he went to Lebanon on a similar peacemaking mission, publicly opposing the dispatching of Korean troops to the Middle East. In the years that followed, he visited many places where people were suffering from war, violence, and poverty: Palestine, Kurdistan, Pakistan, Aceh (Indonesia), Burma, India, Ethiopia, Sudan, Peru, and Bolivia. During these visits, he carried a small camera and began to record the daily lives of the ordinary people he encountered. He carried a notebook for poetry, but in a sense his photos—almost always in black and white—became a major part of his poetic output. In 2010, the first exhibition of his photos was held in Seoul, and in 2012, Culture of Sharing opened the Ra Cafe Gallery in northern Seoul. Since 2010, some three hundred thousand people have visited his exhibitions.

In 2010, Park Nohae finally published a new collection of more than three hundred poems, *Geuroni geudae sarajiji marara* (*So, You Must Not Disappear*), on the themes of resistance, living, revolution, and love. Many poems are based on vivid memories of the poet's childhood or of individuals he met during his travels. Today, living in a remote rural community, he continues to engage in simple farming and to write. A new book is eagerly awaited. He rarely visits Seoul, but he came every week to participate with core members of Culture of Sharing in the candlelight demonstrations that began in October 2016 and finally removed President Park Geun-Hye from office. Most recently, in June 2019, came the opening of a new and larger Ra Cafe Gallery, close to Gwanghwamun in the center of Seoul.

Little remains to be said. Park Nohae was born and grew up as Park Gi-pyeong. Born in 1957 in Hampyeong, South Jeolla Province, in the southwest of South Korea, he grew up in the farming town of Beolgyo, in Goheung County. His father participated in Korea's progressive movements, including the independence movement against the Japanese, and his mother was a devout Catholic. Both greatly influenced him during his childhood. But when he was only seven, his father died suddenly, and his mother, reduced to poverty, found herself obliged to send the children to live with various relatives, while she herself worked in factories.

Virtually none of Park Nohae's poetry has been published in translation. For the world at large, he still remains a faceless poet. In 2021, Culture of Sharing approached me with a request to help translate Park Nohae's poems, since they were eager to make his life and work known overseas. They took some early samples to the Frankfurt Book Fair, hoping to find interested publishers, with no great success. Since then, English translations of the collections *Dawn of Labor, Only a Person Is Hope,* and *So, You Must Not Disappear* have been completed. *True Beginning* remains to be translated in due course. Park Nohae's work is intended to inspire and sustain all who hope for a world of justice, equality, and sharing, wherever and whoever they may be.

Park also wrote a preface to a volume of photos, *One Day,* which featured people from around the world engaged in their daily lives, with poetic captions in Korean and English. He concludes: "All I can and must do with my camera is to recognize, venerate, and love the people of hidden light. My photos and writings are intended to help recognize the true form of the good life and noble humanity found in the ordinary days of ordinary people, and convey a 'seed of hope' to each pure heart."

About Park Nohae

1957

Born in Hampyeong in South Jeolla Province, in the southern part of Korea, Park Nohae grew up in the farming villages of Beolgyo and Goheung. The family atmosphere created by his father, a *pansori* singer and participant in the Korean Independence Movement, and his mother, a devout Catholic, had a great influence on his childhood. Later, his older brother became a priest and served as the leader of the Catholic Priests' Association for Justice, a seminal group in Korea's Democratization Movement, while his younger sister became a nun. The sudden death of his father when he was seven took a toll on Park Nohae's fate. His impoverished family separated, and this early misfortune and solitude made him immerse himself in reading and writing.

1973

Park Nohae moved to Seoul at the age of sixteen and worked at factories during the day and attended Seonlin Commercial High School at night.

1984

At the age of twenty-seven, he published his first collection of poems, *Dawn of Labor*. The collection sold close to one million copies despite the dictatorship's ban, shocking the Korean literary community and the public at large. The pen name Park Nohae, used to avoid surveillance, means "liberation of workers," and from then on, he was known as "the faceless poet."

1989

He formed the South Korean Socialist Workers' Alliance (Sanomaeng).

1991

After being wanted for seven years, he was arrested by the Agency for National Security Planning, an intelligence bureau, and after twenty-four days of illegal torture, he was first sentenced to death and then to life imprisonment for the crime of "leading an anti-state group." He was thirty-four years old.

1993

While in solitary confinement, he published his second collection of poetry, *True Beginning*. Witnessing the collapse of state socialism, he engaged in deep reflection, causing a great stir when he said, "Socialism as a spirit must be preserved, but socialism as a system in reality was wrong. Let us create a new ideology and movement suitable for the changed times."

1997

Still in prison, he published the essay collection *Only a Person Is Hope*.

1998

After serving seven years and six months in prison, he was released under a special pardon by President Kim Dae-Jung, who went on to win the Nobel Peace Prize. Park Nohae was reinstated as a person of merit in the Democratization Movement, but he refused to receive state compensation.

2000

Declaring "I will not live today by selling the past," he embarked on new ideas and approaches to human liberation in the global era. In the face of the four crises facing humanity—the ecological crisis, the war crisis, the global social polarization crisis, and the spiritual crisis—he established the nonprofit organization Culture of Sharing under the banner of "life, peace, and sharing" (www.nanum.com).

2003

Walking the battlefields of Iraq, he continued to promote peace in places of poverty and conflict, holding an old fountain pen with which to write poetry in one hand and an old black-and-white film camera in the other.

2006

Park Nohae carried out peace activities in war-torn Lebanon and built a school in a Palestinian refugee camp. Returning home, he held an urgent press conference opposing the dispatch of Korean combat troops.

2010

Park Nohae's first photo exhibition, *Ra Wilderness*, was held. Focusing on his ten-year journey in the Middle East, the exhibition showed a new perspective on Islam and the region, inspiring deep reflection. Another exhibition, *Like Them, I Am There*, was held at the Sejong Center for the Performing Arts. Over the years, 120 out of 130,000 photos he took in Africa, the Middle East, Asia, and Central and South America have been exhibited. These poems of love and respect, written in light, dedicated to the strong lives enduring in the global village, like tenacious blades of grass, have resonated with audiences around the world. He compiled over three hundred poems written at home and abroad and published his first collection of poetry in twelve years, *So You Must Not Disappear*.

2012

A permanent photo exhibition space was opened at the Ra Cafe Gallery, operated by Culture of Sharing, and over the next ten years, it held 22 exhibitions, attracting 390,000 visitors.

2014

Following the exhibition *Another Way*, a showcase of photos on Asia, held at the Sejong Center for the Performing Arts, Park Nohae published a book of photo essays with the same name.

2019

He published the photo essay book *One Day*, and since then, he has published one book each year: *Simply, Firmly, Gracefully; The Path; My Dear Little Room; Children Are Amazing;* and *Beneath the Olive Tree*.

2020

Park Nohae published his first poetry picture book, *The Blue Light Girl*.

2021

He published a collection of aphorisms, *Reading While Walking Along*.

2022

Park Nohae's first collection of poetry in twelve years, *Seeing Your Heaven*, was published.

2024

Park Nohae published his first autobiographical essay titled *Tear-Flowering Boy*. He is currently writing a book of reflections on the human path in the universe, a book he started writing in prison thirty years ago. Dreaming of the Forest of True People, a community that enables a "graceful life with few possessions," the poet is planting and growing flowers and trees in his small garden, proceeding on a path toward a new revolution.

Follow "Park Nohae's Reading While Walking Along" on Instagram (@park_nohae) and Facebook (@parknohae).

About the Translators and Contributor

Brother Anthony of Taizé

Brother Anthony of Taizé, who also goes by An Sonjae, is a literary scholar and translator living in South Korea. He is professor emeritus of English at Sogang University in Seoul. He has translated more than fifty volumes of Korean fiction and poetry and has written widely on Korean literature. He has received numerous recognitions, including the Korea Times Translation Award, the Daesan Award for Translation, the Korea PEN Translation Prize, and the Order of Merit for Culture from the South Korean government.

Cheehyung Harrison Kim

Cheehyung Harrison Kim is associate professor of Korean history at the University of Hawaiʻi at Mānoa, United States.

Janet Poole

Janet Poole is associate professor of Korean literature in the Department of East Asian Studies at the University of Toronto, Canada.